CONFIDENCE
FEELS LIKE
SH*T!

CONFIDENCE FEELS LIKE SH*T!

ERIKA CRAMER

First published in 2020 by Dean Publishing
PO Box 119
Mt. Macedon, Victoria, 3441
Australia
deanpublishing.com

DEAN
PUBLISHING

Cataloguing-in-Publication Data
National Library of Australia
Title: Confidence Feels Like Sh*t
ISBN: 978-1-925452-30-3
Category: Self-Help/Personal Growth/Memoir

To mami Margie, thank you for always doing your
best, thank you for always fighting for me.
You're my hero ma.

To my darling Hamish, Raven and Navah,
you give me life.

To Jeo, thank you for always being by my side.

Lastly, I dedicate this book to YOU and all the
women in the world who may have forgotten
how incredible, powerful and worthy they are.
In case you forgot your brilliance –
I hope this book reminds you.

Erika is sharing more in her INTERACTIVE book.

See exclusive videos, audios, photos and more...

DOWNLOAD the Dean Library App today and enter the code **CONFIDENCE**.

SEE THIS ICON?

Whenever it appears in this book, it means I've done a podcast on this topic. If it resonates with you or you want to do a deeper dive, head to page 303.

CONTENTS

So, confidence feels like shit, huh?

PROLOGUE

You may be thinking that doesn't make sense.

How can confidence, the thing every woman desires, the thing that helps women achieve more and be more successful, feel like shit? Well...

It's my hope that in these pages, you gain a brand new understanding of what confidence is really like.

I really wanted to give this book this title because it's the absolute core of the work I do every day with thousands of women from all over the world.

There's a truth I always start with, and it is: confidence feels like shit.

In simple terms, the word confidence is defined as "a belief in oneself and one's powers or abilities."

What that definition doesn't tell you is what it actually takes for most women to "believe in themselves and their powers and abilities" – and that's what I hope this book will uncover for you.

I'm going to talk about the real reasons why most women don't feel confident – and don't feel they ever will be.

It's the truth about confidence that not many people talk about (and let's face it, it's not sexy). But once you know this truth, you will be able to create and cultivate the deepest level of inner confidence inside of you – along with a deep self belief that won't be fleeting, but instead, becomes your new state of being.

So, why do I believe confidence feels like shit? Turn the page and let's get started...

WHAT IF THE PERSON STOPPING YOU, WAS YOU?

— ERIKA CRAMER

CHAPTER 1

THE TRUTH ABOUT

confidence

Here's the thing. It's such hard work to become confident, and the journey you've gotta go on to get there is an absolute rite of passage that knows no boundaries when it comes to feeling: embarrassment, shame, discomfort, fear and self-doubt.

It sucks, homegirl. But here's the flip side.

When you create your confidence – and I mean, true confidence – you enter a space where you retain a hundred percent of the power to choose how you feel, what you believe and how you want to experience your life.

Being confident allows you to transcend all sorts of bullshit that holds you back, because it puts you in a place where you learn how to truly let go of what others think, say and believe about you.

The family member who's constantly commenting on the way you parent…The "frenemy" who always finds ways to plant seeds of doubt or tear you down…The mother-in-law who doesn't think you're good enough…The manager or co-worker who criticizes you on the daily…

The opinions and actions of all of these people (and anyone else who you currently allow to have "real estate in your mind") will cease to exist, in terms of how much power, focus and energy you give them.

You won't think about them (at least, not in any meaningful way).

You won't care about their opinion of you.

You won't even care if they – **OMG** – *don't like you.*

> # WHEN YOU GAIN TRUE CONFIDENCE, YOU GAIN THE FREEDOM TO TRULY LIVE YOUR LIFE WITHOUT LIMITATIONS.

Now a special note to all my people pleasers out there who are reading this right now!

You may be thinking: WTF Erika?! How is this even possible? I've lived my whole life worrying about what "they" will think of me.

The reason you won't care boils down to one simple fact: they'll get very little (if any) of your attention. Why? Because you'll have that deep, all-encompassing knowing and understanding that whatever they're doing or saying, or however they're acting, it's all about THEM and the demons they're battling, and it's got nothing to do with YOU.

N O T H I N G. (Feels freeing AF doesn't it?)

When you gain true confidence, you gain the freedom to truly live your life without limitations or constant negativity holding you back, because you become allergic to other peoples' opinions or projections.

Sounds amazing, right? It is! It's a pretty fucking incredible way to live. It's life-changing, in fact. And I know this – because this is how I now live my life.

I used to be a total wreck. I'll share more about my story in the pages to follow but holy shit, let's just say this: I was a hot mess, and then some.

I've been to hell and back in a hundred different ways for a hundred different reasons, and because of that I know what it's like to live in that space of *lack*. Of need. Of craving *validation, love* and *attention*. Of never, ever thinking I'll be "enough" and of looking for love in all the wrong places (over and over and OVER again) in order to fill my cup and make me feel worthy or "good enough."

I've lived with confidence and without it, and let me say this: the path of confidence has the power to change your life in ways you never even imagined.

So, if that's the case, then what do I actually mean when I say that "confidence feels like shit"?

You've gotta admit it's a catchy title! It may even be the reason you picked this book up in the first place. But it's so much more than the name of my book.

It's an ethos. A way of life. And even more than that, it's an invitation for YOU (and women everywhere) to stop accepting less, while also being prepared to put in the hard yards it will take to get the life that you really want.

You know, the one where you actually love who you are.

Where you actually feel in alignment and on purpose.

The one where you only surround yourself with people who light you up.

The one where you get to become the author of your own story, and you get to rewrite any part of it that doesn't work for you anymore.

That life.

So instead of this book being a cute, fluffy, motivational quote or affirmation – I am here to tell you straight up, early on that:

there are no shortcuts when it comes to gaining real confidence.

There is no final destination or place to "get to" where you can tick it off as done!

Sorry sister, there's no sale on "confidence."

It's not something you can order on Amazon.com, add five to your cart, choose overnight delivery and then, tada! *Instant confidence*

Nope. If this were the case, I'd be a gazillionaire.

I would bottle that shit up and sell it to the masses if it were possible.

But, like everything worth having in this life: you gotta do the work.

And you have to be willing to fight for it – because, let me tell you, it's a fucking fight to do this work!

In these pages, you're going to gain a brand new understanding of what confidence is really like – and how it can transform your life.

DON'T SAY I DIDN'T WARN YOU...

Before we go any further, I want to be super, one hundred percent crystal clear upfront: my intention is not to be an asshole and piss you off here.

But I need and want to put it out there, so that you know what you're in for from the very beginning: some of the things I say in this book may piss you off.

I'm sorry, not sorry!

You may want to punch me in the face at times during this book, but trust me; it's in service to you. And I say it with love, I promise…

Side note: there's this thing I've become known for called the **"loving bitch-slap,"** and you may feel this metaphorical slap from time to time when you're reading this book. So, let me explain…it's called "loving" because, first and foremost, I come from a place of deep love and care for you (yes, even if I don't know you). I care deeply about you, and I do what I do because of the obsession that I have for women all over the world standing in their confidence and power.

The "bitch-slap" part is a gentle way of me (metaphorically) slapping you out of your bullshit stories and beliefs that don't serve you.

I have been called "the big sister I never had" by women before, because the work I do is about reminding women like you how incredible, valuable, worthy and important you are – just as you are.

Now, I mean, I'm sure if we met at a neighborhood BBQ or we were introduced at a party, we'd get along really well. Our kids would be buddies and we'd find out we have a lot of things in common, and we'd probably follow each other on Instagram, become great friends, hype each other up and generally love the shit out of each other.

But for the purpose of this book, I don't want to be your friend. I want to be your coach.

Your guiding force. Your challenger and truth talker.

My intention for you is that by the time you get to the other side of this book – by the time you've absorbed the words on these pages, felt the impact of the messages I'm sharing and truly started to understand what you need to do to get in the driver's seat of your life – that you will be committed to doing the work to heal your shit, make peace with your past and create the future you said you've always wanted.

So don't worry, I won't take it personal if you throw this book across the room a few times, or if you all of a sudden "lose" this book for a week or two, as long as you commit to doing this work.

Like I said, confidence feels like shit. It really does. To start practicing confidence, I'm going to push you to *really* do the work. To ask the questions, to go deep, to get uncomfortable and to fully start to understand why you keep getting in your own way when it comes to getting what you want out of life.

That last little comment I made? The one about **you** getting in your own way? That may have pissed you off a little, right? Most women will tell me: "Hold up, Erika, time out. *I'm* not the problem here! It's because of my (insert excuse or blame here), that's why I'm not (insert desired outcome here)!"

This is why I wanted to create this book in the first place: because it all starts with you. The blame. The reasons. The excuses. The responsibility. The opportunity. The choices.

Every aspect of your own happiness, healing and self-worth begins and ends with *you*.

It's up to us as individuals to take responsibility for ourselves and to create the confidence and life that we want. Not just that we want, but that we deserve. And importantly – that we earn. Because once we have true confidence, we have a deep sense of what we want and deserve out of life, and we stop accepting anything less.

We stop allowing toxic people into our lives (and into our kids' lives).

We stop accepting crappy pay for jobs that we pour our heart and soul into.

We stop turning up for others who never show up for us.

We stop letting "friends" treat us like shit.

We stop feeling stuck and bound by limitations that we have allowed to get in the way of what we really want out of life, because we believe we deserve more.

But no one is gonna give it to you! YOU have to fight for what you want in life, and then you have to be prepared to go out there and get it.

This book is my invitation for you to understand that it's your *individual responsibility* to work on becoming a more confident person.

No one is going to do this work for you, so instead of saying…

Just give me the cheat sheet already!

Let me know the secret!

I WANT THE SHORT CUT!

Show me the fastest, least stressful way…

Instead, let's create a REAL and sustainable way for you to change your life. And luckily, I have done it. I am here to be your guide.

I have spent 10 years and literally tens of thousands of dollars doing this work on myself. And let me tell you – it was a fucking shit-show.

This is where you benefit, though, because I'm taking everything I've learned and discovered, practiced and finessed, and I'm packaging it up in this easy to understand, easy to navigate, very digestible (and I might add, pretty damn gorgeous) book.

In the pages that follow, I want to help you acknowledge that although your past and your circumstances definitely impact you, you cannot rise above and create confidence if you continue to point the finger at the things that held you back.

> ## EVERY ASPECT OF YOUR OWN HAPPINESS, HEALING AND SELF-WORTH BEGINS AND ENDS WITH YOU.

That's why there are a number of things that this book is **NOT**.

This book is **not** about women versus men.

This book is **not** about the gender pay gap, although that's fucked.

This book is **not** about the patriarchy, although that's super fucked as well.

This book is **not** about how simple, fluffy and awesome confidence is.

It's **not** about how you "just put on some red lips, girl, put your chinup, chest out and bam, you're gonna to be confident." Nope! Not about that.

This book is **not** about blaming your parents, your trauma, or victimhood* as a reason why you're choosing to opt out of creating confidence and showing the fuck up in your world.

I'm not trying to diminish your experiences, or pretend that you should be able to overcome all your trauma or hard times by just "getting on with it." If anything, it's the opposite – I'm saying all of this to you as a Puerto Rican woman from a marginalized community, who understands that not only did I have being

---

* When I say victimhood, I don't mean to suggest that those of us who have been victimized and had a crime committed against us, should have to gloss over or disregard that pain or experience. What I'm referring to is the behavior – the "poor me" attitude – that keeps us locked into a disempowered mindset from which we feel there is no escape.

an uneducated woman against me, but I had almost all the odds stacked against me.

I'm from a broken, fatherless home; I've experienced sexual, verbal and physical abuse; I've lived in massive scarcity; I've been in and out of foster care my entire childhood; and I have survived more trauma and grief by the age of 25 than I'd ever imagined.

I am speaking from my personal experience here. In no way do I mean to disrespect the things you have been through – the hardships and struggles, experiences and pain. But I want you to understand that every little moment and interaction has created who it is you are today…

They have made you strong, resilient, empathic and wise.

So I don't want you to allow these things to hold you back.

I don't want you to cling on to them as a reason why you shouldn't try.

I don't want you to hold on to a reason why you shouldn't give your life a chance.

That's what this book is not about. It's not about pointing the finger at anyone.

Instead, it's about finding how we as individual women can take our experiences, learn from them, gain wisdom from them and then take ownership and responsibility for creating the life we really want.

Will there be injustice that we come across? Unfortunately, yes.

Will there be assholes who treat us unfairly because of our gender, race, religion, financial status, education, you name it? Of course!

But that's not what this book is about.

Instead, it's about how YOU have the ability to prevail.

It's about how YOU CAN overcome and triumph.

Despite the fact that you may have odds against you – you can create anything and everything you want in this life.

And in a world where there is the potential for so much to be against you, YOU don't need to be against you, as well. There's more than enough that many of us are fighting against, so let's not attack the woman in the mirror looking back at us any more than she already has been.

Can you commit to taking responsibility for you? It's going to be a wild ride, sister, but I promise you – there is the potential for your life to be forever changed.

Let's get it!

CONFIDENCE MUST BE CREATED

Do you think when Beyoncé was born, she came out of the womb positively vibrating with confidence, sass, and self-worth?

Was she an over-confident little toddler, demanding that her needs be met at any hour of the day or night? Well, okay, she probably was – all toddlers are demanding little mofos.

But you get my point. Beyoncé was not born confident. No one is.

Beyoncé, J-Lo, Oprah, Brené Brown – none of them are confident.

Because confidence is not a thing you "have" or a place you "get to."

You can't own confidence.

And like I mentioned before, there is no "confidence clearance" or "fifty percent-off discomfort sale" happening at your favorite online shop.

There is no magical confidence pill, outfit or lipstick color that is going to give you *instant confidence*.

That's just not how it works, sister.

I also want to invite you to stop thinking that confidence is only for some women. That it's only for "those" women. Other women. Women like the superstars I mentioned above – the movie stars we see on screen – the perfectly polished women who fill up our social media feeds.

None of them have the right to be any more confident than you or I do.

And also?

None of them have arrived at "Destination Confidence Town."

Instead, what many of them have done is this: they've mastered the "practice" of confidence.

This practice (which I'm dedicating a whole chapter to later on) is a lifelong practice that once you understand and you commit to, will empower you to be able to create it on the daily. (Yup, it's waaaay better than a cheat sheet.)

The truth is: confidence is not reserved for the celebrities, the pretty ones, the thin ones, the rich ones, the supermodels or the popular ones. Confidence is available to each and every one of us – IF we are willing to do what it takes to create it. The key word here is CREATE; it doesn't just happen. You have to create it for yourself.

I know that it's hard to imagine that Beyoncé or "Jenny from the block" are not permanently confident, but hear me out.

They create their confidence. They make their lives happen.

They. Work. It.

So it may seem like they just "woke up like this," but they didn't.

Although J-Lo does look absolutely incredible – what is she now, 60? 25? Who would know, seriously that woman doesn't age – and yes, she has access to personal trainers, amazing chefs and a home gym, BUT she still needs to do the work herself.

She still needs to haul her amazing ass out of bed at 4am to do her own exercises. She still needs to watch what she eats and move her body on a daily basis if she's going to dance on stage in those 6-inch heels and skin-tight leotard. No one is giving her that – she is doing the work required to have those results.

Results that most women think are only for "some lucky" women. I am sorry to tell you this, but, that just isn't true. If you're reading this right now and you decide you want to be fit, healthy and toned, you can be. You get to chose the kind of results you want to produce.

So, why don't we?

It's far easier and safer to tell ourselves, "Well, you know, I could look like that if I had access to an army of personal trainers, nutritionists, chefs, nannies and the rest. But I don't. So, I won't even try. No, that result is not for me, that's for people like J-Lo."

BULL. SHIT. (This is where our self-sabotage shit kicks in, BTW.)

Why should you have to settle for LESS? And why are you choosing to settle for less in your life, when the power to change is within you?

You have the opportunity to reclaim your power back and you do so by taking responsibility for your current reality and results.

THE POWER OF RESPONSIBILITY

Responsibility is one of my favorite words, and it really clicked for me after one of my favorite teachers, Dr Wayne Dyer, broke it down in a way I could understand.

Wayne describes responsibility in the following way and it's a freaking game-changer:

"To me, the word responsibility means responding with ability. It doesn't mean responding with disability, otherwise the word would be respondisability. No, it is responsibility. I have the ability to respond. I can respond with ability. It means taking responsibility for everything that goes on in your life."[1]

In other words…

Response/Ability is: your **ability** to **respond.**

It's only when you are willing to take responsibility for where you are in your life, that you can actually change it. If you want to feel empowered, take responsibility for your thoughts, your feelings, your actions and your results…If you want to be healthier, take responsibility for how you treat your body and what you decide to put in it…If you want to have more money and abundance in your life, take responsibility for the money stories and beliefs that aren't supporting you and the judgments you have about people with money…

Do you see the pattern here? It all leads back to your **Ability – to – Respond.** And let me tell you, it's deeply empowering.

What's not empowering is pointing the finger outwards as to why you don't have the life you want, the money you want, the body you want, the loving relationship, the job, the house, the car, the lifestyle…the list goes on.

I know it's hard to hear this (trust me, do I know) but if we're going to create confidence together, then as your guide, I have to keep reminding you of your real power.

Of all of the coaching, courses, seminars and people I've invested in and learned from, Wayne has had such a MASSIVE impact on me. I wish I could say I met him in real life – I didn't get a chance to see him before he passed, but his ideas and philosophies have changed my life. He was the one who got me to step down from the throne of "angry Erika, the Puerto Rican chica with a chip on her shoulder" to become more compassionate, less volatile, and way less attached to my ego.

In this book, I will be inviting you to consider many different views that you may not have already considered and I'll be sharing the big ahas, teachers, mentors and exercises that changed my life.

I want to challenge you here because I know that being seen as a "confident woman" has not been easy for me, or the many women I have coached and studied over the past decade.

I am gonna keep bringing it back to you throughout the book because there is only so much you can "control" (and I use that word lightly).

Let's break it down a little here…

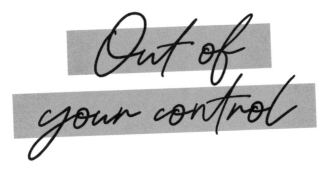

Out of
your control

- 👑 How other people see you and think of you

- 👑 The past experiences you had

- 👑 What other people say to you

- 👑 The way you were raised

- 👑 How others react or act around you

- 👑 How other people behave

- 👑 Other people's beliefs

- 👑 Actually – other people (basically anyone except you)

In your control

- 👑 How you choose to see yourself

- 👑 How you choose to think about yourself

- 👑 How you choose to feel about yourself

- 👑 How you choose to act around certain people

- 👑 How much of your life you choose to share with others

- 👑 How you react to/around others

- 👑 How you treat other people

- 👑 The situations and outcomes you're willing to put up with

- 👑 The end results you get in your life

No one,
Nothing

HAS POWER UNLESS
YOU GIVE IT POWER.

YOU GIVE IT POWER
BY BELIEVING.

NO BELIEF.

NO POWER.

ERIKA CRAMER

There is a lot in your control.

And I want us to focus on THAT (remember, if it's in your control you have the ability to respond).

But where do you think most of us focus all of our energy and attention?

OTHER PEOPLE AND THE PAST.

The shit that is NOT in your control.

Let me be clear about what I mean when I say "other people": I'm talking about what they think, say, believe and do (and to all the mamas out there, yes, your kids are other people).

When I say "the past" I mean what has already happened to you (or as I like to say, FOR you). Again, most of us spend all of our time focusing on what happened in our past, worrying about the past and thinking that what happened back then will happen again. It keeps us rooted in fear and its bestie, anxiety.

When my husband died in 2007, I became rooted in fear. When I got remarried, I spent every evening worrying about my current husband dying as well. If he didn't walk through the door when it got dark outside, my mind would go straight into the story of my past, "He's crashed, something bad has happened, I can't become a widow again…"

This obviously didn't serve me and it wasn't reality. I was living in fear of my past and projecting it into a future that by the way, never came true!

Can you see why I invite you to focus on what you can control? This is where you'll need to go within. You will need to strengthen yourself. You will need to constantly remind yourself of what you can control on this journey of becoming a confident, responsible creator.

Practicing confidence is hard because practicing presence is hard. It's uncomfortable, it's confronting and it requires deep excavation of self.

The deepest.

So I want you to think about the reason why you picked up this book…(note that these answers will be the anchors that keep you coming back to your why).

- Where do you lack confidence or self-belief?
- Where do you keep doubting yourself?
- Why are you constantly going to the worst-case scenario?
- Why do you put limitations on yourself and your life before you even begin to explore an opportunity or change?
- Why do you care so much about what others have to say or think about you?
- How often do you find yourself comparing yourself to other women?
- What's up with all of the negative self-talk and the inner critic who puts you down on the daily?

If you were in my office or at one of my live events, these are some of the questions I would ask you to journal on.

And after coaching thousands of women from around the world on creating confidence, here's my guess as to why you're not striving to live your very best life:

You don't want to put yourself out there for a fear of messing up.

You don't want to be vulnerable in case you get hurt (again).

You don't want to go through additional pain or discomfort.

You don't want to be rejected.

You don't want to be judged.

You don't want to be wrong.

You don't want to get hurt.

You don't want to fail.

Therefore, you play small. You stay playing it "safe."

You don't do the scary shit that you know will get you what you really want, so you make up all sorts of excuses as to "why" you can't get or do what you want.

Therefore, you keep getting the same crappy-ass results, you then complain about it to the same group of friends who ALSO lack confidence, have a fear of failure and don't want to be seen.

Let me share with you a little snapshot of a life I used to live; see if you resonate with any of it...

This is what my old "friends" and I used to do when we would get together: we'd complain about the areas where life wasn't fair. The shitty boyfriend who never helps around the house. The partner who always has time for his friends but never has time for me. The mediocre job where I worked so hard, but I was never appreciated for my efforts or ever paid enough to do all the work I did.

I would get together with my "friends," drink cheap-ass wine, bitch and moan and then repeat the same cycle the following week.

"

PRACTICING CONFIDENCE IS HARD BECAUSE PRACTICING PRESENCE IS HARD.

"

Nothing changed. Maybe, just maybe, that's because we all held onto the parts of our lives that didn't work, because it was easier and more comfortable to just stay there, complain, play it safe, and be reassured by each other that we had every excuse under the sun to compromise and accept less because, you know, life is hard, right girl?

For some of you reading along right now, this is resonating like a motherfucker. (I can almost feel that nod of recognition). For others, it might be making you feel frustrated or uncomfortable. You may even be angry at me for suggesting that YOU may be playing it safe and small because it's the path of least resistance. And that maybe, you fear leaving your comfortable, familiar life behind…and that you could be scared of what might happen if you take flight?

If you really try. If you actually succeed.

But you know what? That's okay! I'm okay with you possibly having a reaction to what I'm saying because it means you're really starting to question your own situation and your beliefs, habits and choices.

So, consider this one of many **loving bitch slaps** I've promised to give you throughout this book, in order to help you push past the self-doubt and have some serious "aha" moments to propel you forward.

WHEN I...THEN I...

Speaking of moving forward – I want to talk about the "When I, then I" bullshit.

It's that shitty way of thinking that prompts you to think about the future – at the expense of living in the present.

It's that bullshit that stops you from feeling happy, fulfilled, or enough NOW and prevents you from ever having what you actually want.

It's also a total waste of time.

It is the myth that says your life will improve and you'll gain more confidence and everything will just magically fall into place "when" something specific happens.

Does any of this sound familiar?

"When I finally meet the right partner, they'll make me feel loved, validated, adored and supported and I'll start to feel really good about myself. And then, I'll be more confident – and when I'm confident, I won't worry about what others think about me anymore, and all of my problems will go away, because confidence is the gold star I should aim for so that I can feel AWESOME and carefree like all those 'confident women' out there…"

NO. Fucking. Way.

It's time to bust the B.S.

You can insert anything into the above "When I, then I" myth.

When I finally lose weight…get a higher-paying job…start my dream career…meet new friends…live in a bigger house…buy a better car…earn more money…find my purpose…get a six pack… live closer to my family…live further from my family (haha!)…

Whatever it is that's personal to you; it's the myth that when something external happens in your life, you'll finally be happy and because you're happy, you'll have more confidence in yourself.

Reality check: you can choose to BE happy and confident now.

Then, you would DO the things that confident people do and you'd HAVE the results that confident people have.

You just need to choose to BE confident.

I want you to think about your answer to this question:

If I were confident right now (meaning, if I was already confident) what would the confident version of me do?

Well, she would take action.

She would probably do the scary shit you've been avoiding. She would go for what she wanted because she knows that she is the only person who can determine her future and therefore her happiness…

Is this starting to make sense? Getting your dream life doesn't make you confident, it's the other way around: becoming confident means you're more likely to go after your dream life.

So why aren't we all just BEING confident? Why aren't more women like you choosing confidence over this "When I, then I" crap?

Because confidence isn't comfortable.

Comfortable is safe.

Confidence isn't created in your comfortable safe zone.

Therefore it's not easy.

It's actually hard work.

And most of us are not willing to show up in this (scary AF) way.

And if you ask me, this is the reason why I believe most women don't go there and therefore they don't identify as confident. Because they want it to be easy – and it's just not.

THE DANGER OF PLAYING IT SAFE

You cannot create confidence, self-belief and courage by playing it safe.

Confidence is all about doing the scary shit (the pee dripping down your leg shit).

It's about feeling overwhelmed.

Dancing (sometimes boxing) with self-doubt.

It's about overcoming your inner critic (who can be one sassy ass biatch).

None. Of. This. Is. Meant. To. Be. Safe!

AND P.S. What's so good about safe? Safe is boring AF! The incredible life you want to live and create isn't safe – it's exciting! It's intentional and it's out there…waiting for you to show up and make it happen for yourself.

Think about all the times you mustered up the courage to do the thing you were scared to do or to have the difficult conversation that you know needed to be had.

Think about all the times that you felt the fear and did it anyway.

This is what being confident truly feels like. We don't talk enough about the practice and the process of confidence and I hope that I can help you gain a better understanding of what "being more confident" actually means.

Instead of you wishing for more confidence I am hoping this book helps you go out and actually have the tools to **create** it for yourself. I feel like when we want something badly we don't always get it in the way we think we will, either.

I remember wishing to be a more patient driver. It seemed like every time I got behind the wheel, I was surrounded by idiots on the road, and I'd get so frustrated by being cut off by people who were apparently unaware of this thing called a turning signal that came with their car.

The more I wanted to be patient and accept that I can't change the ridiculously terrible drivers around me, the more it seemed that I was faced with even more really annoying people cutting me off on the road and not using their signal when turning (oh girl, that still pisses me off!).

The only way I was really going to gain more patience for my fellow "challenged" drivers was to be challenged by them! And it worked; I am so much calmer when I drive and I don't allow others to make me feel any type of way. I get to choose how I want to react.

I believe confidence is the same.

I believe that our desire to stand in our confidence, to own our voice and reclaim that powerful part of ourselves means that we are ready to make some scary choices. To do things that aren't so "safe."

To actually be activated and initiated into our deep self-belief and inner power like the Queen that each and every one of us is.

THE PRICE YOU PAY

Having everything you desire, creating life on your terms, loving yourself inside and out, doing work that lights you up, having all the abundance and love you can imagine – all of this sounds so damn incredible, right?

And yet…you think it should be a walk in the park? You think it should come with ease?

Since when has anything we deeply desired been "easy"? If it were easy, then you wouldn't value it. If it were given to you, then you wouldn't know the actual cost of what it took you to get it. And you wouldn't fiercely hold on to it and protect it at all costs, once you have it.

As a mother of two, I now find myself struggling to find the balance of loving my two boys so much and giving them the world, while also knowing how much hardship I went through in my childhood and how it made me so resilient and strong. How do I teach them about struggle and pain without them going through it? How do I teach them how to be with their sadness and their self-doubt, without them moving through those emotions and those moments themselves?

I can't. They need to feel it. They need to move through it on their own, they need to experience pain and learn how to heal it. And that's hard to think as a mother, but it's the truth.

And it's true for you in your journey to self-belief and unshakable self-confidence.

I can tell you hand on heart that the woman I am today is because of all the hard things I had to go through. And although I rarely sit in the space of self-doubt nowadays, I can tell you right now that when

I do, I know it means I am up-leveling to the next version of myself – a version that is going to be even more capable, confident and able to handle whatever life throws at me.

The tough emotions are designed to move us in the direction we are asking to go in.

I want you to know that I am going to take your hand along this journey of you creating your confidence, but I need you to promise me that you will continue.

That you won't give up on yourself when it all feels too hard.

That you won't opt out of showing up.

That you won't go back to playing it small and staying comfortable.

That this won't be another personal development "self-help" book that "didn't work." Or something you "binged" but didn't action.

I want you to promise me that you will keep moving forward, against the odds, even when it's hard – knowing that what waits for you on the other side is so worth the journey it takes to get there. 👑

CHAPTER 2

I SHOULDN'T *be here* RIGHT NOW

You cannot create *confidence*, *self-belief* and *courage* by playing it safe.

— ERIKA CRAMER

EP #39

Before we go any further, I need you to know why I'm so obsessed with doing this work around transformation. The woman I was a decade ago is truly unrecognizable compared to the Erika of today – and I want to tell you a bit of my story because I want you to know that **I get it.**

I get what it's like to doubt yourself and feel like you're not good enough.

I get what it's like to feel like no matter what you do, you'll never be enough.

I get what it's like to experience loss and feel completely alone.

I get what it's like to suffer with shame, guilt, abandonment, loneliness, anxiety and fear.

I get it.

When women see me on social media or come to one of my live events they usually think, "Oh, it's easy for you Erika, 'The Queen of Confidence' – it must be so nice to be so positive and confident all the time." But that's actually not the case.

It wasn't (and it still isn't) "easy" for me. It has actually been the hardest thing I've ever had to work on. I had to become greater than my environment and I had to transform every adversity I was faced with.

I had to learn how to shift my perspective on the shitty cards that life had dealt me. I had to change my perspective on how I saw my life and what I chose to focus on.

This is a choice we all have.

And the reason why I need to share my story with you is because, if I am honest – I really shouldn't be where I am right now. I technically "shouldn't be" living the incredibly amazing life I am currently living.

I actually thought I'd end up pregnant multiple times to multiple men, addicted to drugs and/or homeless.

But that wasn't my reality. I didn't allow my fucked up past to create a shitty future. My past doesn't get to define who I become.

And that's why I want to tell you about it.

I want you to know that YOUR past, your pain, your hardships and traumas do not have to define you.

Instead, you can stand in your story and find the gifts in your hardships, the lessons in your suffering and draw on your inner strength in order to create the life you want to experience.

What I'm about to share is really important. Not just because I want you to know my story, but because I need you to understand that when I tell you to "reclaim your confidence," to "stop letting your past determine your future" and to "take responsibility for healing your shit" – all of this comes from my own experience doing so. I walked the talk sister.

So as cute and pink as this book is, and as nice as it may sound to call myself the Queen of Confidence, don't get it twisted.

There were a lot of dark times where I didn't know how the hell I would get myself out.

I can't tell you every crazy story that I've been through in this book (there's another book coming for that, don't worry!). But I can share with you how my story began, and some of the milestones along the way that shaped the person I am today.

I hope that you see yourself in my story; maybe the pain, suffering or hardship resonates and I hope the lessons I got come through for you as well.

I was born and raised in a little city located 20 minutes outside of Boston, Massachusetts. My mom became a single mother when my dad left us, when I was two years old. Having been diagnosed bipolar, my mother suffered with manic episodes where she would stop her medication and get really, really sick.

During her manic periods, she would become physically and verbally abusive. Throughout my childhood and teen years, my mom was in and out of mental hospitals and I was in and out of the foster care system, living with different foster families.

She would stop her medication and after three days, she'd become manic and really paranoid. Out of nowhere, she would start hitting me non-stop until the neighbors would call the police. I remember one time, before I'd even started school, we both ended up arrested with handcuffs on our wrists and ankles. As we were thrown into the back of a police car together, I was yelling and swearing at the cops (I was a very hot-headed, take no shit kind of five-year-old!).

I would get placed into a foster home and my mom would get put in a mental hospital. Mom would get sick like this at least twice a year.

And just in case you're wondering, my mother and I have an incredible relationship now. She is my hero – I mean, to raise a child on your own, living on food stamps, while battling with a mental illness…I can't even imagine. She suffered so much yet she NEVER gave up on me and she never stopped fighting to get me back.

Being in the foster care system was tough, as you may know; these systems in most countries need work. Although I loved living with other kids and changing schools and being in large groups, this is where my sexual abuse began. This is where I lost a lot of my innocence.

This back and forth, unstable upbringing led me to growing up as a kid who had anger issues – I was constantly defending my mother and her behavior on the playground during recess. I got into a lot of fights, I doubted myself a lot, my grades always suffered, I didn't believe that I was good enough or smart enough and I felt like other people didn't like me. I ended up having major abandonment issues and would get into trouble at school daily.

When I was seven years old I was kidnapped by my dad when my mom and I went on a family vacation to Puerto Rico (and that's a whole other story…). When I was finally reunited with my mom the following year, we jumped back into the same cycle of mom getting sick, me visiting her in mental hospital and living in yet another foster home.

Moving into high school I struggled the most. I would skip school and not show up to class, and I ended up fist fighting with anyone I could pick a fight with in the hallways. I had a permanent seat in the detention center of every school I transferred to. I became hard, harsh and cold. I would tell people: "I'm good, it's all good, I am fine. I don't need to get all emotional, soft and sensitive and talk about my feelings."

"

I HAD TO LEARN HOW TO SHIFT MY PERSPECTIVE ON THE SHITTY CARDS THAT LIFE HAD DEALT ME. I HAD TO CHANGE MY PERSPECTIVE ON HOW I SAW MY LIFE AND WHAT I CHOSE TO FOCUS ON.

"

I tried to protect myself with anger and violence and being the "tough girl." But the reality was, I was sad, lonely and I felt like I wasn't good enough, smart enough or worthy of anyone's love.

That obviously didn't serve me moving into adolescence and at 17 I ended up joining the Army due to my grades being horrendous and my mom being poor – there was no way I'd get an education, go to college or make something of myself without the Army (or so I thought at the time).

The Army had offered to pay four years of any state college or university to anyone who signed up in high school. Funnily enough I never went to college; they ended up paying for my hair school tuition!

My senior year in high school, I was off to bootcamp. I ended up being in the US Army for 10 years (eight years' active duty, my last two years inactive) and moved across the country, marrying my high school sweetheart Jeo in secret as he went off to fight the war in Iraq, as he too joined the military in high school.

The year he got back from war, I decided I would put my dreams and desires on hold so we could chase his goals; after all, he went from high school to the Marines and hadn't really done anything else in his life. I felt so guilty that he had missed so much "life" being deployed in the Marine Corps and felt it was his time to shine.

So, I suggested we move from California to Florida so he could study and live his dream of being a music producer and DJ.

I was 21 years old when we moved to Florida. And this is where my first major "holy fuck" moment begins…

LIFE MAY BE TOUGH RIGHT NOW. BUT REMEMBER: YOU'RE TOUGH TOO.

ERIKA CRAMER

GOING 152MPH

When I was 23 years old, I woke up in the emergency room of the Orlando Regional Medical Center to cold scissors sliding against my thighs.

There were a group of medical professionals hovering around me and someone was cutting my jeans off my legs. That really woke me up – those were my $80 Express jeans! At the time, they were my most expensive piece of clothing and it had been a massive splurge.

Why was someone cutting them to shreds?!

In the background, I could hear my husband Jeovanni screaming and yelling. The lights got brighter and my awareness became stronger. He was arguing with the hospital staff, but I didn't know why; it seemed as if they were holding him down.

Immediately, I began apologizing: "I'm so sorry, he's not usually like this, please! I am so sorry."

Can we just take a moment to acknowledge how messed up my mind was back then, that even when I was lying in a hospital bed, confused, disoriented, bloodied, broken and bruised with no idea what was wrong with me – I still cared more about Jeo and I upsetting the nice hospital staff than I cared about what I was doing in the hospital in the first place?

It turns out I should have been more worried about my body and why there were so many nurses around me, because my situation ended up being pretty serious. I had fractured my back and crushed my left ankle. I had barely made it out alive from what was the most horrific drinking and driving car accident I had ever known of.

A few seconds passed, and I blacked out again. Jeo went into a coma for 12 hours after that, as he had severe head trauma. And I woke up in a dark hospital room that morning, in a haze, still unaware of what was going on, but slowly realizing that my movements were restricted and I was in a very, very bad way.

Some nurses came in moving their lips but I couldn't make any sense of what they were trying to say. They handed me a pen and a clipboard and one of them assisted me in what was an appalling attempt at signing my name.

I blacked out again and the next time I woke up, my vision had slightly improved. I could see someone standing in the corner of the room: it was Virma, my Army supervisor, aka SSG Lopez.

The doctor was there and proceeded to tell me that I had fractured my back in two places and that the bone was damaged so badly, they needed to fuse it with titanium. My left ankle needed hardware to repair it as well.

"You're very lucky," he told me. "If you had been in any other position when you crashed, you could have been paralyzed permanently."

"Accident? What accident?! Surgery, what are you talking about? What happened to me?"

I was in total shock, as I still had no idea why I was in hospital.

At that moment, my memories started flooding back in snippets and bursts. *Oh, fuck.*

Jeo had been driving. Earlier that night, we'd been invited to a nightclub in downtown Orlando with some friends who had a VIP booth. We had no money to spend on drinks and no money for gas, but there was just enough in the tank to get us there and home. Besides, they had a VIP booth so that meant free drinks. "Fuck it!" Jeo and I had decided. "Let's go have some fun."

At the end of our "fun" night, we got into the car to drive home. Now, I don't know how or why we made the decision on this night to get behind the wheel of the car (or how the hell the bar staff even let us leave the venue, as drunk as we were) but I do remember that when Jeo sat in the driver's seat and his friend got in the front passenger seat, I demanded in my drunkenness that they both put their seat belts on.

I climbed into the back seat, right in the middle – which is where I planned to hover over them so I could make sure "we were all safe"…yet I never put a seat belt on myself.

Sounds like some shit a drunk person would do huh?

Yup, I was wasted.

Jeo was wasted, and his friend was too.

The car we were driving was a red Mitsubishi Lancer Evolution – you know, the car from *The Fast and the Furious Part 2?* Jeo's parents had bought it for him when he returned from Iraq as a "welcome home" gift. If you know your cars, you know that this one happened to go really fast. Also, these cars don't have a speed safety chip, which usually limits the speed a driver can reach before it prevents the car from going any faster.

This car went 152mph (or 240kmh) with no chip.

You can imagine what happened next.

We took off and then we all fell asleep – at what point I am not sure. What I do know is that we fell asleep in fifth gear, going the max speed the car could go.

I woke up seconds before we crashed and well, it was too late. As our car was headed straight into a ditch, my vision went black.

We smashed into a ditch, which turned the car so we were facing backwards. We hit a van that was parked in the lot of a convenience store, and the van pushed us into a tree, which then smashed us against the convenience store brick wall.

I was later told that the Jaws of Life came to break the car open so they could get Jeo out and they took us via helicopter to the nearest emergency room.

After a 12-hour stint in a coma, Jeo was thankfully fine. His friend walked out with a fractured rib, which was a miracle.

I was broken and battered beyond belief.

I had broken my back, but more so, I had broken my spirit.

DID I JUST GET A SECOND CHANCE?

As you can imagine, my recovery after this accident was brutal. I'll spare you all the gory details, but I was in the hospital for almost a month, permanently attached to a morphine pump to numb away the excruciating pain.

When they pulled my initial bandages off, I felt like they opened my entire back up. I screamed in agony.

If it felt like my hospital stay had been 25 days of hell, then I was in for a rude shock when I returned home. Learning how to walk again was a nightmare and trying to pee without a catheter in me was painful. But the worst part was that I hadn't even started my recovery and healing journey.

The three months to follow were the three months that began to change my life.

In many ways, I was literally starting again: I had to develop the mental resilience to learn to walk on my own with no walker, to be able to shower with no assistance. Being able to walk to the front door unassisted was one of my goals.

It was baby steps towards getting my life back again.

But I was determined that I didn't want my OLD life back. I wanted a new one.

Was this a chance to hit the restart button?

A moment to work out if everything I was doing was what I actually wanted to do?

It felt like it. Something shifted in me at that point.

I knew I had dreams, goals, wants and deep desires. But it had never seemed like there was a chance in hell that any of it was in my reach. I felt like I had wasted my life being in the Army: what was I there for?

To do what? That wasn't my dream!

Since the age of seven, I've always wanted to be an actress and performer. (I still do!) I wanted to perform. So I started imagining a life where I stepped in that direction. If I wanted to be J-Lo, what was my first step going to be?

Getting rid of my ratty-ass regrowth, for one.

I asked Jeo to take me to go and get my hair color done. I was blonde at the time with two-inch regrowth. I was swollen and broken and I couldn't walk, but damn it, I was determined to look better than I felt.

So, off we went to the hair salon and the solarium. Afterwards I left feeling like a million bucks. I wanted to do something to help me look better, because I felt like if I looked better, I would feel better about myself. It sounds ridiculous but it's true; sometimes you need the boost of a physical "pick me up" to get you in the right frame of mind.

That little trip to work on my outer self gave me the confidence to start working on a new goal. I wanted to be an actress but I couldn't just expect to walk on set and book a movie star role; I had to start small. I thought modelling could be a gateway into performing.

There was a different future out there for me: I could see it. Feel it. Taste it. I slowly put myself out there, showing up, taking risks and making moves towards the life I wanted to create.

I began emailing photographers from my bedside table. And I began booking jobs: as I recovered and got stronger, I was hired to appear in music videos with famous rappers and I was booked to shoot covers of bikini magazines.

Eventually I was working full-time in my Army unit as my day job, I had started hair school at night (to help me transition out of the Army gig) and on weekends I was modeling and doing music videos in Miami. It was such a crazy time. I remember locking myself in my office, hiding from my Army supervisors so I could do a phone interview for an article in *FHM*.

I may have paused my life before this accident and it felt like not being able to walk made me want to RUN. So the minute I could get to creating my new life, I was all over it.

It took a near-death experience to give me the push I needed to go after (what I thought were) my dreams in life.

Here's the thing: I was determined to change my life and I knew the old way wasn't working, but at that time, I wasn't doing the work that I needed to do in order to actually get different results.

To be honest, I didn't know what "working on myself" even meant back then. I thought confidence was all about looking good then feeling good. Act the part, then the feeling of confidence will follow!

I had no idea.

My life did change and I was feeling more motivated and excited about my future than ever, but it was like this surface level of happiness.

It wasn't until 2012 when I moved to Australia that my real growth began, but I do look back on this car accident and breaking my back as my first real holy fuck, AHA moment.

It was the first experience I'd had in my life that really shook me, woke me up, screamed in my face: ERIKA! YOU HAVE ONE SHOT AT THIS LIFE!

Why are you wasting it?

Did I really need a near-death experience to realize that I wasn't happy or fulfilled?

Apparently so. My hope is that you don't.

You don't need to wait for shit to hit the fan – to realize that your life is precious and worth living to the fullest. You don't need your life to come crashing down in an epic moment of fate or being faced with – death, divorce, debt or disease before you make much needed changes. Instead of waiting for shit to happen to you, you can make shit happen *for you*.

You don't need
to wait for a near
death experience

TO REALIZE YOUR LIFE IS PRECIOUS

and worth living
to the fullest.

— ERIKA CRAMER —

Earlier, I briefly mentioned Virma, my amazing Army boss. When I broke my back in the car accident, she was truly an angel to me. I couldn't tell my mother as I feared she would get too stressed, become mental unstable and possibly get sick again (she had gone three or so years with no mental breakdown, and I didn't want to be the reason she ended up back in the hospital).

Virma was the only person I had at the time. She treated me like her daughter, she sat with me, bathed me, fed me and nursed me back to health. She drove an hour every day to be with me in the hospital – she was literally heaven sent. I honestly don't know where I would be today without her.

She was there for me the day I almost died in a horrific car accident.

And she was there for me a year later, when I found myself back at the hospital, this time waiting in a cold, sterile room, again wondering what the fuck was going on?

It was a Sunday afternoon. The night before, Jeo and I decided to have a house party to celebrate Cinco de Mayo; there was a big pay-per-view boxing match happening between Oscar De La Hoya versus Floyd Mayweather, so we invited our closest friends together for some drinks.

We had such an awesome time, in the safety of our own home, drinking, eating and having great conversations with our friends.

I had work the next morning – once a month I had Army duty on a Saturday and Sunday – so I decided to slow the drinking down and by around midnight, I went to bed.

The next morning I woke up in fear, thinking I had overslept. I turned to see that Jeo wasn't in the bed next to me. I picked up my phone and saw he had called me at 1:20am. No text, no voicemail? I quickly got up thinking he may have passed out on the couch, but he wasn't there.

I started getting ready as I was running late and walked out in the living room. I saw his two friends sleeping on the couch, but where was Jeo?

I woke them up as I was still getting ready and trying to figure out where he was. One of his friends said he had left late last night to give one of our friends a key he had left at our house. I was so confused because we'd had a house party – we weren't going anywhere. After the accident, we'd promised to never, ever drink and drive again. It didn't make sense – why did he leave our house to return a key to someone?

At this point I was worried that maybe he'd fallen asleep in his car outside in the parking lot. I told his friends to look for him and that I'd check back in. I was really late now so I rushed off to work. On my way in, I couldn't stop thinking of where he could have been.

When we finished our morning formation, I went to find SSG Lopez (Mama Lopez). I told her we had a party last night and Jeo wasn't home when I woke up. She told me not to stress, and to keep calling his phone and that maybe I should try calling some hospitals or prisons, just in case.

His phone kept ringing, which gave me hope.

Maybe he's fallen asleep at the drive through? Back at our apartment his friends were looking at the usual places he may be.

At 11:45am it started raining. I looked out the window and wondered: where are you Jeo?

By this point I was panicking. I told Virma that I was scared that he may be somewhere alone and that by now we should have found him.

Needless to say, she let me go. I drove back home and met with his group of friends, praying the entire drive home that I would walk in the door and see him sitting on the sofa, looking sheepish, with some crazy story that he fell asleep at a friend's house…But no luck.

At home, I checked my house phone and noticed that the hospital had called at 7am. That was weird. The hospital calling wasn't the weird part – the year before when I broke my back, the surgery had set me back over $120,000 that I didn't have, so they were constantly calling to chase money.

They never called that early, though. I called the hospital back. I asked if they had anyone by the name of Jeovanni Lopez there and said that someone had called me at 7am.

"Ma'am we're sorry, we can't give you information like this over the phone, it's probably best that you come in."

I was worried but honestly, in that moment, what it sounded like was: "We don't know what or who you're talking about, but if you think you'd like to double check, come in and let's see if we can help you."

My worst fear at that point was that Jeo might be at the hospital and worst-case scenario, he might have some bandages around his leg.

I'll never forget the moment I walked into the emergency room lobby. My eyes locked with the young man at the front desk: he was the same kid who I had spoken to on the phone 20 minutes earlier.

"Hi, I'm the woman who called looking to see if my husband was here, his name is Jeovanni?"

He looked at me, then looked down and nervously asked me to please wait in the waiting room "over there," as he pointed his finger at the private rooms near the ER double doors.

These are the rooms where they tell you the "news."

I instantly felt sick. Inside the room, I was pacing.

They kept me there for what felt like hours and I had to keep asking for answers. "Can anyone tell me anything??" I was getting fed up with waiting to find out where my husband was, but worse, I began to get really scared. It was torture.

Across the room from me in another one of those waiting rooms, out came a little elderly lady – she was an angel. She could see how flustered and upset I was and she tried to reassure me. "My dear, it's okay, these rooms are just to give you some privacy – my husband is having heart surgery and I have been here waiting too. It's going to be okay darling."

She soothed me and gave me hope. She helped me feel calm and gave me an ounce of peace. It didn't last very long, though.

CONTROL ALT DELETE

After I'd been waiting for what seemed like an eternity, I'd had enough. It felt like I had been in that room for days, so I was about to march over to the front desk again and demand some answers. I looked up and noticed the double doors to the ER swing open as if it was all in slow motion.

I locked eyes with a nurse in bright blue scrubs, and then a doctor in a tan suit jacket with clipboard in his left hand.

As soon as our eyes met, their gaze dropped.

The nurse spoke first. "I'm so sorry. He didn't make it."

Time stood still. I heard the words, but I couldn't comprehend what she was saying.

I stood up.

Again, the nurse spoke. "I am so very sorry. We did everything we could."

It felt like an eternity passed while my brain tried to catch up.

Finally, I was able to ask. "What do you mean? He didn't make it? I don't understand?"

"Jeovanni Lopez, your husband, he didn't make it. I am so sorry, we tried everything," she repeated.

In the background, I could hear his friend Ryan wailing, sobbing, screaming as he fell to the floor.

But I had no words. No feeling. Nothing. It was a void.

Literally, that was my moment of pure insanity. It's like when you are so shocked and dazed that you don't actually know what reality is. Nothing made sense. Nothing felt real. It was like a deafening stillness and silence in between words, in between breaths.

I was in another dimension where the silence felt like an eternity.

I have never felt so still, so frozen and so numb.

"I don't understand, I am sorry, but I don't understand? What do you mean? I don't understand?" I kept saying, over and over again.

Until finally it sunk in, and I snapped. I was still wearing my Army uniform. I ripped off my jacket and threw it across the room and screamed at the top of my lungs. I picked up a lamp and smashed it against the wall. I fell to the ground.

The nurse and doctor picked me up and tried consoling me. And instantly, I went back to the blank state, eerily calm and frozen.

I remember saying that I didn't know what I was supposed to do.

"What do I do? What am I supposed to do now?"

The nurse said, "Oh honey, you don't have to do anything. We're so sorry for your loss."

On Sunday, the 6th of May 2007 at 4:35am, my husband Jeovanni Lopez had passed away while drink-driving. He veered off the road hitting a ditch and flipping his car.

He wasn't wearing a seat belt.

When I tell you that to this day, this single moment has been the hardest, most excruciating thing I've ever had to live through... Not the physical abuse, not the jumping from foster home to foster home, not the sexual abuse, or being kidnapped by my father, not breaking my back or Jeo being sent to war for a year...none of it could compare to this deep loss.

I went into the hallway and laid on the floor, where I sobbed and wailed at this reality that I really couldn't accept or understand. He had been in a car accident. He had died. My Jeo had died. Nothing made sense.

I called Jeo's mother. When she heard my voice on the phone, she screamed: she had been under the impression that I too had died in the car with him. It was horrible. Surreal.

Enter Mama Lopez, who at the time was on her way to Mississippi for a mission with the Army. I called her in a shambles and this woman stopped in her tracks, turned her car around and once again came to my rescue. She got the Army to give her permission to be on emergency leave with me.

Virma had saved my life again.

She came and she looked after me. She stayed with me.

I now know the universe has sent this woman to guide me because the series of events that I was about to move through, I could have never done alone.

I mean, I was in full depression, full insanity mode. I was doing all seven steps of grieving at once. I don't even know who I am, where I am, what the fuck day it is. What's going on. I don't understand. I don't understand why I'm stuck. I don't understand why my husband is gone. Is this real? What the fuck is going on? Where are you? Like, Jeo, are you coming home? Is this a sick joke?

Anger, sadness, grief – I was feeling all of it at once.

Most of us say we could never go through something like this but the reality is that when you are faced with these difficult times, you somehow find a way to keep showing up. You have to – you don't have a choice.

This was my rock bottom.

I had lived through so much pain and adversity and trauma, but this? This I couldn't work through. I had never known anyone who died and to have my husband be my first experience of death felt like an injustice. I felt completely trauma'd out – like, fuck me, haven't I been through enough? Now I have to deal with this, too? I was positive that God or whoever was in charge, hated me.

The next five years were a blur. I got into relationship after relationship that didn't serve me, just so I wouldn't feel alone. I took on modelling jobs so I could feel desired, pretty and worthy.

I numbed out for the next five years of my life, trying to Control ALT Delete my past and basically doing anything I could that would make me feel less broken and damaged. And I hate to admit it, but I kept drinking and driving. I was desensitized to the extreme. I didn't want to "deal with it," whatever that meant, because I had a deep-seeded unconscious belief that if

I let myself cry too much or "deal with his death," that I too would become bi-polar like my mother – and I didn't want that to happen.

To be honest, I didn't even know how to "deal with it." I'm not sure if you've ever felt that way, but it's a weird space to be in. You know something's not right, you know you're not a hundred percent fulfilled and happy, yet you have no idea how to fix it, or what to do about it?

And the pain didn't end there, the series of events that I had to go through once he passed away only added to the suffering. Going to the morgue to identify my husband's body, having a private wake, dealing with all of his family (who didn't even know we were married, because we got married in secret before his first deployment overseas – my God.)

It was a lot.

DOWN UNDER

In 2009, I ended up meeting a man at a hair conference in Las Vegas. He was Australian and he was completely different to anyone I had ever dated before: different accent, different style, different upbringing. Australia was a place that had never, ever been on my radar. I didn't even know where it was!

I fell in (what I thought was) love with this guy and decided that this was my ticket to a new life and clean slate.

I could start again and leave my past in America – because apparently the shit you sweep under the rug in one country won't follow you to another, right?!

WRONG.

I packed up my entire life and moved to the other side of the world for this man. And do you know what? All my skeletons, trauma and unresolved pain followed me across the Pacific Ocean.

Who would have thought!

I had moved to Australia to start a new life far away from home, with a man who ended up being no good for me – I had attracted a man who confirmed what I felt about myself. That I was not worthy. Not good enough. I was damaged goods.

I put up with so much shit in that relationship and was so deeply home sick and unhappy.

But, I was determined to make Australia work. I remember calling Mama Lopez and telling her about the failed relationships and feeling so embarrassed that I had left so abruptly, asked her to sell my car and all my belongings because apparently "he was THE one."

I refused to just go back home for fear that everytime I would see a kangaroo or hear about the land Down Under I would cringe and think about that failed relationship. No way, I didn't want to leave Australia on those terms. I knew there was more to this magical and beautiful country I was in.

"

WHEN YOU ARE FACED WITH THESE DIFFICULT TIMES, YOU SOMEHOW FIND A WAY TO KEEP SHOWING UP. YOU HAVE TO – YOU DON'T HAVE A CHOICE.

"

So here I am at my lowest of lows, living in Australia, thousands of miles away from home, a single widow with no friends – feeling oh so sorry for myself. And literally the only two people I had in my life at the time were: my nail technician and my personal trainer, Hamish.

Seriously?! My service providers were my only friends?!

I had dedicated myself to working full-time and going to the gym daily in order to help me out of the "eat pray love and tubs of ice cream" cycle. Hamish and I developed the most incredible friendship. He was on a journey of self-development and he was like no man I had ever known before. He was soft and gentle, but strong and masculine – he was so kind and seemed so self-aware.

He had coaches and mentors and he believed in the universe, manifestation and positivity. I had no idea about spirituality back then.

I literally followed his lead, his very gentle invitation. He cared for me so kindly and he listened to all my stories, and he was the first person I told my life story to – ALL of it.

He loved me and accepted me for who I was and everything I had been through, he helped me celebrate Jeo's life and make peace with the grief. It was incredible (it still is incredible) to have a man like him truly care about me.

In the summer of 2014 Hamish and I were married.

It was the happiest day of my life.

He introduced me to his coach Tanja (who is now my dearest friend and soul sister). She was my first ever life coach and mentor and with her support, I went deep into ALL the pain, suffering and trauma I had swept under my rug over the years.

It was a bumpy ass ride with lots of emotions and challenges I had to face (at times it was unbelievably painful), but after coaching with her and other incredible mentors over 12 months, I completely changed my life.

It led me to going deeper into my stories, my pain and my healing.

Hamish and I spent over $100,000 (and counting) in those first 10 years of healing. We went on retreats, had private and group coaching, saw healers, business mentors – we did it all. And in case you're wondering, I came to Australia with a maxed out credit card and got more credit cards to finance all of this.

Hamish refinanced his home and we found the money wherever we could to continue to invest in our growth, healing and development.

We found ways to put that first and we made huge sacrifices (we didn't even have a wedding!) and to this day we continue to find ways to keep growing and up-leveling our mindset, our spirits and our relationship as lovers and parents.

My journey to self-development and healing has been the best investment I ever made because it opened my eyes up to the truth: I was living in the victim space for most of my life. I was not aware that my thoughts, my feelings and my actions were creating my reality.

I had been living at the effect of what happened to me, the "poor me" mentality and repeating those patterns over and over again.

What I didn't realize is that my traumatic childhood experiences had influenced so much of the mindset that I had cultivated.

Until this day, one of the most important tools for my incredible transformation was learning how to shift my mindset. 👑

STOP WORRYING
ABOUT FALLING.

WE ALL FALL.

IT'S ABOUT HOW YOU
GET BACK UP AND
NOT MAKE A BIG DEAL
ABOUT FALLING
IN THE FIRST PLACE...

JUST KEEP MOVING.

ERIKA CRAMER

CHAPTER 3

CREATING A
confidence
MINDSET

EP #19

It's time for a little check in. I know that last chapter was a bit heavy. (Okay, maybe a lot heavy!)

But I needed to share that with you. I find that so many of us see confident women and we instantly assume that they've got their shit together. Or that they're the lucky ones, the chosen ones, who simply get to be confident because that's the card they've been dealt in life. They're gorgeous, glamorous, outgoing, witty, bubbly – of course they're gonna be confident, right?

That's not how this works. And the truth is, we compare ourselves to others without ever really knowing what that woman may have been through to get to where she is now.

That's why it's so important to me that you have an understanding of where I've come from, because it's been a long-ass journey to become the Erika I am today.

And before we get into practicing confidence, I need you to be across a few more things…

My number one goal as a confidence coach is to teach you the most important, life-changing concept ever (nope, it's not how to be confident). It's how to manage your mind. Why?

Because it ALL starts here.

Everything I talk about and teach you in this book will all lead back to your mind, and the stories you're *choosing* to tell yourself and believe (or in some cases *not* believe) about yourself and others.

If you're going to learn how to create confidence, you need to learn how to manage your mind and create a confidence mindset. You'll also need to learn how to stop giving a fuck what others think of you – or as I like to call it FWOT (fuck what others think – more on that later).

These two things are the simple but powerful strategies you're going to use to start reclaiming your confidence and standing in your power for good.

Now, I briefly mentioned in the last chapter how I was unaware of the power of my thoughts and how my thoughts were creating my reality. Understanding this became the key to my transformation and something I am excited to share with you, because they form the foundation of how to create confidence. It's the number one thing that led me to healing my traumatic past and realizing that I had a chance at *actually* changing my life.

I know how much this work can help you, no matter where you are and what you're faced with. All that is required is a desire to *want* to feel better.

Until I started working on myself, I had lived most of my life as a (wholly unconscious and unaware) victim. Instead of having a confidence mindset, I had adopted the "victim mentality." As I've mentioned already, this is not a dig at being a victim – I lived my whole life being victimized. This is different.

When you understand the meaning behind victim mentality or victimhood, you see that it refers to a person who is living at the *effect* of their life.

You become someone who uses their past experiences (usually a trauma or injustice) as a reason why you cannot create a different outcome for yourself. Here are a few examples from my own life and childhood about how this can manifest…

👑 My father left my mother and I when I was two years old, so I grew up angry and untrusting towards all men.

👑 I grew up as an only child and never had any siblings to bond with, and that's why no one gets along with me.

👑 If it wasn't for my mother being sick all the time, I would have got better grades in school and actually gone to college.

In all of these statements, I'm laying the blame on other people. Although those things may not be my *fault*, it is my *responsibility* as a grown-ass woman to work on those beliefs so it doesn't continue affecting my life or my future. Or worse, so I don't pass that shit onto my children as well. Is this making sense?

All of these statements may have some truth to them.

But they don't serve me!

When we choose to point the finger outwards as to how it's "their fault" or other people's responsibility as to why we don't have what we want, **WE** lose. Not them.

And remember that if we don't take our responsibility back, then we can't make the important and positive changes to our lives.

Let's flip those statements above around and see what they could be if I take a more active, responsible stance:

👑 My father left me when I was two years old; in reality I have no idea what was going on for him at the time, but it doesn't mean that all men are untrustworthy.

👑 I grew up an only child and never had any siblings, which means I was able to develop some sister-like relationships with my girlfriends growing up and ended up learning how to easily get along with strangers, thanks to being in foster care throughout my childhood.

👑 If it weren't for my mother being sick all the time…honestly, I still wouldn't have gone to college. I was never very interested in studying and I realized that I had no true desire to go to college (besides living the college party life, that would have been cool for a few weeks after high school!)

VICTIMLAND SUCKS

The victim mentality is the disempowered mindset that led me to living in Victimland for most of my life.

I set up a tent and camped out in Victimland, eventually got my citizenship and made it my home. Actually, let's be honest – I was the fucking Mayor of Victimland. I bought land, bought property and had a pity party with all my negative neighbors on the daily.

I lived in Victimland for such a long time. I didn't even know there was a way out…

Nowadays, I don't spend much time if any in Victimland. I mean, I might do a layover in Victimland. I might stop there briefly because I'm having a moment, but then I'm like, "Oh shit…Oh yeah, I know where I am! I'm in Victimland and I don't like this fucking place. But I clearly need to be here right now – let me feel my feels, have a pity party of one and then get the hell out of here."

I've been there a lot. I used to go there a lot as a kid, I used to be there a lot as a young adult in my shitty relationships. I used to reside there permanently, until doing this work.

If you don't commit to working on your shit you don't even know you live in Victimland. Some people were born and raised there, they put their kids in school there and they die in the Victimland cemetery! Okay, this is getting out of hand now isn't it? But hopefully you get what I am trying to tell you! If you're ready to leave Victimland – the good news is, you can.

It starts by shifting your mindset.

You see, your mindset is everything. When I realized that I could choose how I wanted to react and that my **thoughts** created my

feelings, which then impacted my **behavior** and the **action** (or lack of action) I took, which led me to the results I got in my life…

Everything changed.

It wasn't until I learned the concept of "your thoughts create your reality" that I actually started understanding my patterns (thanks again, Wayne Dyer).

You can't cultivate confidence when you believe the thought that you're unworthy and not good enough.

You can't go for that promotion when you keep believing the thoughts that you suck at your job.

You won't attract the partner of your dreams when you keep believing the thoughts about how you're too old, too fat, too broken, too "something" to find love, and that you'll be single forever.

When I first became a stylist, I would help women dress for their body shape. I would take them shopping, choose incredible outfits with them and help them look and feel amazing on the outside.

I kept coming across women who lacked confidence in themselves and who didn't feel good about their bodies, so I thought: easy, I know what you need!

Let's get you some nice clothes, change your hairstyle and teach you how to put your makeup on – this would fix all their problems, right?

Sure, it did – for about 10 minutes. Unfortunately, it was only a Band-Aid.

Instead of culling their wardrobes, I needed to be culling their thoughts.

It's like those "skinny" jeans in your wardrobe that don't actually fit you, but you keep them in there with the hope that "one day" you'll be thin enough, good enough and pretty enough to actually fit

"
YOU BECOME
WHAT YOU
BELIEVE,
NOT WHAT
YOU THINK.
"

— OPRAH WINFREY —

into them again. Those asshole jeans sit there as a reminder of how you're "just not there yet" in terms of being the "best" version of you. In fact, every second those jeans are allowed to take up space in your closet, they make you feel worse and worse about yourself.

Thoughts are the same. Although we don't always choose what thoughts pop into our mind, we can choose not to attach ourselves to the crappy stories and we can choose what we're going to believe. If you don't clean up the wardrobe of your mind, these bullshit thoughts will run your life.

LIVING ON AUTOPILOT

It's my intention that you get to know your own mind in this chapter. It may seem like a strange thing to say to "know your own mind," but the reality is most of us don't know our minds (this is why big corporations pay millions for marketing, and why we the consumers spend so much on things we don't necessarily "need").

We don't know what we're thinking most of the time, or how it's causing us to feel. And we don't know that we are actually in control of whether or not we want to believe the shitty things we tell ourselves.

Most of us don't actively choose – let alone question or inquire into – what we think. We respond from the subconscious (our autopilot program) and instead of leading with our own thoughts, we react and end up stepping back into our learned or borrowed patterns and behaviors.

So much of our life is spent on autopilot. It's actually our brain's way of being efficient. We are running on an automatic program most of the day.

(If you're anything like me, you may enjoy this break down. Remember, I sucked at school and I had no idea what any of this shit meant when I was first learning about it. And I am really passionate about breaking shit down).

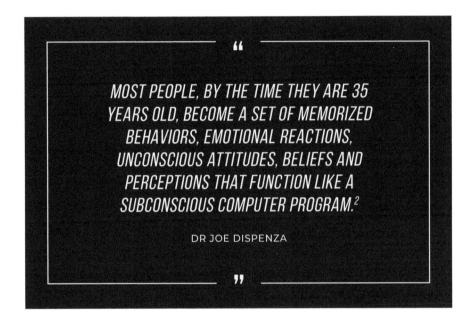

"

MOST PEOPLE, BY THE TIME THEY ARE 35 YEARS OLD, BECOME A SET OF MEMORIZED BEHAVIORS, EMOTIONAL REACTIONS, UNCONSCIOUS ATTITUDES, BELIEFS AND PERCEPTIONS THAT FUNCTION LIKE A SUBCONSCIOUS COMPUTER PROGRAM.[2]

DR JOE DISPENZA

"

IF YOU **DON'T DEAL** WITH YOUR SHIT...

YOUR SHIT **WILL DEAL** WITH YOU.

ERIKA CRAMER

1. CONSCIOUS = AWARE

To raise your consciousness means to become more aware. To be conscious is to be paying attention, also known as "awareness."

As you're reading this, take a deep breath then let it out...That was you deciding consciously to do that (thankfully you don't need to tell your body to breathe).

2. SUBCONSCIOUS = AUTOPILOT

This is the part that allows us to drive to the grocery store, talk on the phone (hands-free) to a friend, chew gum and also tell our kid off in the back seat, all at once while driving. This all happens on its own (scary huh! Sometimes I'm like, who drove my car?! I don't remember driving the last ten minutes at all...) and studies show we spend ninety-five percent of our time in this autopilot mode.

Although this may be useful for daily tasks like brushing your teeth, driving to work or wiping your ass, it's not useful when it comes to your negative beliefs, handed-down and learned fears, or the need to constantly please people. Autopilot is something I lived in for years and I was so incredibly miserable.

3. UNCONSCIOUS = UNAWARE

I see this as the dark basement of our minds, where no conscious awareness exists (think deep trauma and memories that you may have forgotten about). You have to actually go down there and actively seek it to find it.

In my therapy years I was able to find memories just by talking to my therapist. In recent years I was also able to access the unconscious successfully with modalities like NLP and hypnotherapy.

> "
>
> IF WE DON'T CONSCIOUSLY PLANT THE SEEDS OF WHAT WE WANT IN THE GARDENS OF OUR MINDS WE'LL END UP WITH WEEDS.
>
> TONY ROBBINS
>
> "

The important one here is the subconscious, because we're actually operating from this space most of the time. If we don't commit to understanding where the "autopilot mode" switches on then we'll fall into old patterns of thinking and feeling over and over again.

If you have "always lacked confidence" or always identified as "shy" and you don't commit to doing the work on it, then those same patterns will lead you to the same mediocre results that you don't want, but that you keep getting.

When it comes to managing your mind and creating the life you desire, you'll need to commit to becoming much more aware of your current thoughts. You'll need to find and then break the autopilot programs that don't serve you, in order to re-wire (literally) your brain for confidence, success and the living embodiment of a creator who makes shit happen for herself…are you excited yet?

There's huge power in just one basic, underlying concept here:

YOU. GET. TO. CHOOSE.

You get to choose what thoughts you engage with.

SWEEPING IT UNDER THE RUG

So many people want to avoid working on their mindset and looking at their negative or uncomfortable thoughts, and I truly believe this is why.

I like to use the analogy of a living room rug.

We spend our whole lives "sweeping shit under the rug" and wearing masks to cover up how we *really* feel. (Shit, I used to have a full zip-up bodysuit to cover up my feelings!)

Then one day, after shoving all the skeletons, the shame, discomfort, guilt and grief under the rug, you realize it's so lumpy and full you can't even climb over the damn thing. It's like climbing a mountain in your living room (depending on how much you've been avoiding your thoughts).

Then one morning you try and run out the door, but the bony hand of one of your many skeletons grabs your ankle.

"SHIT! Get off me!" you try to shake it off you, because you don't want to face that bullshit – it's uncomfortable, it's too painful, too raw.

"No! I can't do this right now. I am fine, everything is fine." *(Plasters on the fake smile mask).* "I don't have time for this anyway, I can't do this, everything is fine, none of this matters anymore, I am totally okay and totally over it, can't I just move on and act like none of this ever happened?"

Does any of this sound familiar?

It was definitely my reality for many years.

And we wonder why we have all this deep seeded self-doubt, lack of worthiness, lack of trust, low or no self-confidence, etc.

We gotta deal with our shit sister, or our shit will deal with us.

This doesn't mean you have to sit in therapy for five years by the way. (I was in therapy from the age of four. I spent 19 years in therapy and I still had stuff to deal with).

But you do need to make a commitment to yourself to continue working on you.

When I take my clients back to their childhood memories, we don't do it to "relive the past" or to "go through" that experience again –

we do it in a neutral way that allows them to visit that part of their experience that maybe hasn't had closure.

It's incredible what intention can do. When you have an intention to connect with yourself and you close down your eyes and get still, get quiet – you'll be surprised how healing *just that* can be.

Many times, we think our past experiences aren't a "big deal," yet they continue to affect us in adulthood. I'm not just talking about the big stuff, either – small, subtle, seemingly inconsequential experiences and situations can have a lasting impact.Your parents fighting or splitting up; being bullied about your weight at a young age; being told you're weird; being made fun of for any reason – all of this can be trauma that creates a wound and ends up really messing with us in adulthood.

Doing this work allows you to acknowledge, reveal, heal and gain lessons and closure from your past experiences.

I know – it doesn't sound like much fun. But you can't disregard your core experiences growing up. Because all of these foundations make you, you – good, bad or ugly.

The experiences from your upbringing are some of the most significant predictors of how you view yourself in adulthood, and therefore how you make your way through life.

I know all of this can feel a bit heavy, but I can't fluff this shit with you. If you're going to become more confident, learn to manage that mind and #FWOT, then you need to know what you're really getting into.

Let's unpack a bit more about the basic way our minds work.

When I started doing this work I was SO blown away, I did a deep dive into so many different modalities that my coaches and mentors were teaching me. I became obsessed with the breakdown as it gave me a tremendous amount of awareness and freedom (if you geek out on things like this the same way I do, don't worry – all of my juicy book recommendations and resources are at the back of this book!)

First, you need to understand that thoughts are popping into your mind at all times (experts say we think around 60–70,000 thoughts per day, holy crap!) plus eighty-five to ninety percent of those thoughts are recycled from the day before AND to top it off – you're unaware of what you're consciously thinking around ninety-five percent of the time (ha ha, there's a reason this shit is called "doing the work.")

So what happens when you have a stressful thought?

Well if you're like me and most of the women I have worked with in the past, you usually become aware that you have a FEELING, an emotion pops up (you may feel sad, angry, defeated, anxious or "not good enough.")

Most of us will say we FEEL a certain way, but we don't usually go: "I am THINKING this particular thought."

The reality is that THOUGHTS are what create FEELINGS and FEELINGS then create more THOUGHTS.

And because we're in autopilot mode and so unaware, we don't even know that we feel this way because of our thoughts.

This is the key – when you FEEL a way you gotta find the

THOUGHTS that are leading to this feeling (and trust me, there is a thought – or 46 of them), and once you discover the thoughts, you'll be able to unravel it all.

EP #22

I CREATED MY OWN REALITY

Here are some common thoughts that popped up for me when I decided to go to the beach with my husband six months after my first baby was born:

I am so fat and disgusting.

I am pale and so unattractive.

I can't believe I've let myself go.

How could I do this to myself?

I am not sexy any more, my husband doesn't love me…

DAMN, Erika! I mean, can you feel the emotions that would follow after those shitty thoughts came rushing into my mind?

Those terrible thoughts were stories that made me feel incredibly horrible, and who I became in the moment was a woman who was suffering because she was believing her bullshit thoughts.

The **FEELINGS** that followed those **THOUGHTS** above were as follows: I instantly felt angry, unworthy, defeated, disgusting, hopeless, self-pitying, sad, resentful, and not good enough.

Now back to how our mind works, once we get the **FEELINGS** in response to the thoughts – this then leads to a **Behavior** – usually an action, a reaction or a lack of action (and it keeps feeding us even more negative thoughts).

So there I am at the beach, feeling so shit about myself, watching my husband Hamish with his incredible 72-pack, wishing that I could just disappear.

So what did I DO? What was my **Behavior**? I became passive aggressive, I got snappy, I made him out as the bad guy, I complained about the sun, the wind, the sand – you name it, I was over it and we had just got there!

Not only did I react and snap at Hamish when he tried to get me to go in the water, but I spent the entire time sitting in the tent with a grumpy ass face on, eating all the chips and sandwiches we had packed – AND hating on the beautiful women in bikinis, while Hamish and the baby had the time of their lives.

Next comes the **RESULT**.

In my example? Well, it doesn't feel great to sit at the beach, feeling shitty and inhaling half a bag of potato chips all by yourself! Afterwards I felt bloated, sick and even more sorry for myself. Plus my moodiness only pushed my husband away more and he ended up just letting me be, while he had a blast with the baby.

Which reinforced exactly what I was thinking about myself to begin with, right? As this whole process leads back to the original thought: "I am so fat and disgusting, I can't believe I let myself go, my husband doesn't think I am sexy…"

Are you getting this? It was next level when I learned about this process, so:

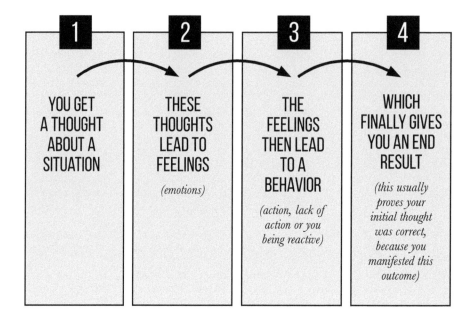

It's so important for you to know this information – and not only know it, but apply it.

And here's the amazing part: if you recognize that you can *pay attention* to your thoughts and feelings and then decide to *choose a better thought* – or investigate and inquire into that thought (instead of blindly believing it) – then you can actually create a different and more empowering outcome.

For example: "I feel so fat and disgusting and I've let myself go" can instead be "I am not feeling the best in my body right now, but I just had a baby and my husband loves me. I am learning to embrace my post baby body and right now, I am choosing to enjoy this day at the beach."

CONFIDENCE FEELS LIKE SH*T

I can choose to feel good, grateful and excited about our family day at the beach, instead of focusing on my own insecurities and projecting them onto my husband.

And I can choose to believe that just because my body doesn't look how it did pre baby – it doesn't mean I'm fat, lazy, unsexy or destined to be overweight forever?!

Then I can be present with my amazing family and enjoy the sun and our beautiful beach trip! I can play in the water with my new baby and amazing husband.

The end result = lots of fun and great family memories.

The choice is ours.

The problem is that for many of us, we don't even realize that we allow our thoughts to take over. We then feel crap about ourselves as a default setting. And if that's the case, then how can you ever CHOOSE a different outcome?

YOU CAN'T.

Here's an exercise I do on the daily in my journal. You can also do it on a scrap of paper, or a Kmart receipt – it doesn't matter!

Whenever I'm not feeling my best (this could be overwhelmed, anxious, sad, chaotic – basically an emotion that doesn't serve me), I take a pen and I start writing how I feel. I spill my EMOTIONS on paper – these are words like:

I am so: angry/defeated/overwhelmed/lost/confused/irritated/worried/disappointed.

Then I ask myself:

- ♕ What are the thoughts that are running through my mind?

- ♕ What am I thinking about right now?

- ♕ What am I telling myself about myself?

Next, you let yourself write. Don't judge what comes out! 'Cause let me tell you – if you're truly honest with yourself and you purge your thoughts freely, some shit is going to come out and it's most likely going to make you deeply uncomfortable!

"

THE CHOICE IS OURS. THE PROBLEM IS THAT FOR MANY OF US, WE DON'T EVEN REALIZE THAT WE ALLOW OUR THOUGHTS TO TAKE OVER.

"

I let myself write that shit down so I can get it out of my system, and more importantly I can see the thought, investigate it, work out whether it's serving me or not, how and where it came from, then put it in its rightful place (most often, my mental trash can).

For instance, I once wrote this down when I was journaling: "My kids are holding me back in my business."

Harsh, I know. Is it true? No! But in that moment, is that how I felt? Yup! This was a time in my business when I felt angry, pissed off, not cared for, misunderstood and frustrated.

Then I realized I was overwhelmed and I felt under-supported from my husband, because I had failed to ask him for help (communication breakdown on my end).

I was having the thought about my kids, then this one popped up: "I'm overwhelmed and my husband is useless." That thought wasn't true, but my feelings were valid, and I needed to communicate how I felt.

Consider this: what kind of wife do you think I was being when I was in this frame of mind? When I was believing this bullshit story? Do you think I was talking to my husband with kindness, respect and openness? Or was I walking around with this angry, pissed off, aggressive autopilot chip on my shoulder?

The latter…

I took the thought. I created a story around it and subconsciously decided to act that story out, and it quickly became my reality. Because I was being bitchy and rude and passive aggressive, that's the person my husband reacted to – and then he himself became less understanding, less helpful and less open to checking in with me.

This is what happens if we don't question our thoughts. If we don't allow ourselves to get out how we feel, we believe the stressful stories that are swirling around in our minds. And that's what they are ninety percent of the time – stress-inducing stories!

AN UNQUESTIONED MIND IS

the world

OF SUFFERING

— BYRON KATIE —

HOW JOURNALING HAS CHANGED THE GAME

Okay so stay with me here, even if you may be thinking: journaling? Seriously?

Before you say "Erika, I hate journaling" or "I just can't get into it," hear me out.

When I suggest journaling, what I really mean is that you make a time and choose a place where you can have some space and silence to allow yourself to let your thoughts out of your mind, and put them on paper. Think of it like verbal diarrhea, only on paper (you're welcome).

This is not some "dear diary" shit either. And there's no airy-fairy, "write three things you're grateful for" script you need to follow (although practicing gratitude is very powerful too!).

It's really just a simple practice you can commit to daily in order to help you clear your mind.

It's a chance to do an inventory of the thoughts that are in there swirling around and, most importantly, it's about creating a space where you have freedom to let yourself express what's coming up for you – filter and judgment free.

I don't care if you're writing in a fancy-ass journal or you're scribbling notes on the back of a receipt, there's no judgment here.

As long as you commit to writing, that's all that counts.

I want you to get to know your own mind.

It starts by getting to the bottom of the top three to five thoughts that mess with you the most.

Here's some prompts to get you going

👑 How do I feel in this moment?

👑 What am I thinking right now?

👑 What's the statement in my mind trying to tell me?

👑 When did this feeling come up?

👑 What happened before I felt this way?

👑 Is this a thought I think a lot?

👑 Where did this thought come from?
Is this something you picked up from a family member or a friend?

👑 Is this thought what I really, actually think?
Or is it an old pattern response?

Your top three thoughts that hold you back. Do you know what they are? If you don't, I highly recommend you start now.

Because once you know what they are you'll have the power to bring them into your awareness and start working on creating more empowering thoughts.

I call this being the "Sherlock Holmes" of your mind – because you are inquiring about your own mind and thoughts. It's a really simple yet effective way to "reverse engineer" how you're feeling, so you can figure out what just happened and why you feel crappy now.

I talk to myself (like *all* the time) and one of the many questions I ask myself daily, out loud, is: "How do I feel right now? What's going on? I don't like how I feel…I'm frustrated or cranky or short-tempered or annoyed. Why do I feel this way? I need to investigate…"

Usually, I can track it back to:

- A conversation or experience I've recently had with someone else

- An article or post I read online that triggered a reaction

- A memory or a reminder about something I "need to do" that I don't really want to do.

Or a variation of the above.

The bottom line is, whatever it was, it got me in a mood – and if that goes unchecked or undiscovered, my whole day can go to shit!

Can you see why so many of us keep doing the same things over and over and getting the same results?

Can you see why paying attention to your own thoughts is absolutely crucial if you want to change your life?

WHO'S GOT THE REMOTE?

What happens when you start to pay attention to your mind is pretty remarkable. You start to gain a deep level of awareness. You start to notice how many times per day you doubt yourself, you second-guess yourself and you think a shitty thought about yourself.

You start to notice how much you judge yourself – and others.

You start to realize that your mind is spending way too much time in a false "future," and way too little time in the present moment. You start to realize how much you unconsciously go to the worst-case scenarios in your mind.

Mainly, you start to notice how much fear, anxiety or anger has been controlling your life.

There's a movie I recommend to all of my clients and it's not really something they expect from me, as it's a kids movie. It's Disney PIXARs *Inside Out*, which is a film about a little girl who experiences some childhood challenges.

Predominantly, it's a real look at how our minds work.

In the movie there is a control panel in the little girl's mind, and there are characters who take over, depending on what's going on in her life. Although JOY is in the mix, JOY rarely gets to run the panel. It's way more frequent for FEAR, DISGUST, SADNESS or ANGER to be running the show.

The reason I love this movie so much is because it prompts you to think: who is running the control panel of MY mind?

Have you ever thought about that?

And what if you had the remote control, meaning you could choose who is sitting at the control panel?

I hate horror movies. I used to watch them as a kid all the time (I am pretty sure *The Exorcist* has scarred me for life, I'm not even kidding).

I watched them so much and would get so fearful that still to this day, if I wake up and have to pee at 3am, my heart races a little (and yes, I may still be a tiny bit scared of the dark).

If I hate horror movies so much, why did I keep watching them?

Beats me!

But it's a perfect analogy for what so many of us do every day with our own minds.

I want you to imagine that you are just like me and you hate horror movies. Yet, there you are watching the horror channel 24/7. You don't like it one bit but when you get that remote control, you go straight to the horror channel. You want to change the channel to a love story or a romantic comedy but somehow, you end up back at the horror channel again and again…

You talk about how much you don't like it.

You complain about how horrible and scary it is.

You pledge to make some changes. Yet, you don't change the channel!

YOU have the remote control.

You could easily change it to a comedy. But every day, you sit there in fear, hands shaking as they slightly cover your eyes, shivering while wishing you could watch something else.

This is what managing your mind gives you: the ability to take the remote control and purposefully, finally change the damn channel.

IT'S TIME FOR A RENOVATION

I love me some analogies (as if you can't already tell), so before we move on to the next section I want to share one last activity with you that is going to help you look at your mind in a whole new light.

What I want you to do is to imagine your mind as if it were a house.

We are all born into our circumstances; we are born into a family, a country, a city, a certain gender, maybe also a religion and/or a set of guidelines that shape our upbringing. You have absolutely no control over this.

You grow up in this environment, which you didn't get the chance to choose (well, I do believe we choose our parents but that's definitely a whole other book!).

And whatever life has thrown at you determines your outlook on life, and the way you perceive and interact with the world around you.

Let's say you were born into your family and you were born as a girl. The fact that your family had a girl means something to them; in some cultures or families it would be celebrated as the highest honor.

In others, it may be less desirable to have a daughter. There may be a cultural predisposition as to how your family and society treats you. Depending on the country and religion or beliefs of your family, that can impact the way you interact with the world, too.

Let's say: you're a girl from Australia and your family is Christian. Already, this means *something*.

It means you will be raised the way that they believe is the best, according to a certain set of rules and guidelines that they have chosen.

You didn't get to choose the values and beliefs and ideologies and inclinations that they gave you.

If they are people pleasers (because that's what their parents unconsciously handed down to them): they will teach you about being a "nice" girl, and how to go through life without grabbing attention or being too loud or too outspoken; because "nice girls should be seen and not heard" (I threw up in my mouth there just a little).

If they are middle class: they may teach you about the value of hard work, and why you need to go to college and study hard to "achieve something." There is no Plan B – it's work your ass to the bone or bust.

If they are of a certain religion: they could encourage you to pursue relationships within the same religion.

You get where I'm going here, right?

You have no control over it and you get this family – whether you love them to bits or you can't stand them (or a bit of both at different times), it is what it is. You are born into your circumstances and this is the "mind" (aka the house) you inherit.

Your parents (or whoever raised you) bought this house, and they decorated it over the years with their own thoughts, beliefs, ideas, experiences and values.

So this house they have given you (your mind) has been fully decked out by them according to their taste.

They chose the city and the suburb, the neighborhood and the street.

They chose the specific house and the number of bedrooms it has.

They picked wallpaper for the walls, the carpet under your feet, the tiles in the bathroom…

I WILL NOT
LET ANYONE
WALK THROUGH
MY MIND
WITH THEIR
dirty feet.

— MAHATMA GANDHI —

They hung curtains and chose the lighting and they even picked out the furniture and the décor.

Then YOU lived in it all your life.

> ## WHATEVER LIFE HAS THROWN AT YOU DETERMINES OUR OUTLOOK ON LIFE, AND THE WAY YOU PERCEIVE AND INTERACT WITH THE WORLD AROUND YOU.

It's all you've ever known, the house you grew up in. But this house might be constructed of beliefs and ideas you fundamentally don't agree with – and ideas about life that really don't fit with how you want to live anymore.

And maybe now that you're grown, you're starting to realize that some of the things you think and believe aren't necessarily true... (also keeping in mind that your parents cared about you, and I'm sure they did the very best they could with what they knew).

Your parents, your upbringing and your childhood created the habits, beliefs and thought patterns you have now. It's subconscious, second nature. And unfortunately during your upbringing, there were seeds sown for some of the damaging self-chatter we perpetuate as adults...

If I'm quiet and keep my room tidy, it won't trigger my dad and he won't get angry and lose his temper at my mom = as an adult I'm a people pleaser.

If I try my hardest, work my butt off and go the extra mile wherever I can to get good grades and help others, then my mom will stop comparing me to my super-smart brother = as an adult I bend myself into a pretzel to get other people's approval and validation.

If my older sibling always fucks up and causes mom and dad stress, then I'm going to be the good girl, toe the line and do the right thing = as an adult I'm always nice, compliant and "easy-going."

I think you're getting my analogy now!

What I want you to take from this is that maybe you need to re-decorate your house (your mind!). You can keep some stuff – the good lessons and beliefs that shaped you into the woman you are today. But you can also decide to get rid of all the other crap that doesn't serve you anymore.

Maybe you need a full-on renovation! Maybe there's a lot you're discovering in this chapter, and you need to get a bulldozer and start from scratch. But just like a real renovation, you don't need to dive in and do it all at once. You can start slowly, for example: upgrading the kitchen first (untangling yourself from the toxic relationship you have with your mom).

Or you could re-tile the bathroom (address that bitchy competitive streak you have with your siblings).

Or you could rip off that nasty ass wallpaper in the hallway that has the "you should care what people think of you" written all over it.

Or maybe, you want to start by working out the things that you really **love** and want to keep in your house, like the beautiful lamp your grandma gave you (she always told you how loved and special you are, which makes you value and share unconditional love with others you care about).

It's a powerful way to look at your mind and realize that YOU CAN change your thoughts, and therefore change your reality.

It all starts with awareness and inquisitiveness.

And it leads us to…What if?

What if the thoughts or stories you grew up believing were not real?

What if they were just scary stories handed down from generation to generation?

What if there are beliefs you are holding onto unconsciously, and they don't reflect how you really feel or who you really want to be?

What if you are hanging onto beliefs and ideals that don't make sense for you?

What if there are things you have been conditioned to "believe" and they're just not right?

What if…you don't have to accept the "house" you have been given as the one you're going to live in forever?

This is the beginning of your renovation – right now. Today.

It could be a fresh coat of paint, or it could be a full knock-down and rebuild.

But it starts now. And it starts with you.

WHAT IF THE THOUGHTS OR STORIES YOU BELIEVE ARE NOT REAL?

WHAT IF THEY ARE JUST SCARY STORIES?

ERIKA CRAMER

THE LIFE-CHANGING FOUR QUESTIONS

As you can probably imagine, it took me a lot of **work** to get to where I am now. I had a whole construction crew working on not only renovating, but also relocating, my "house" to a brand new country! And that's a perfect word for it: *"work."* There have been no shortcuts to reach this place of empowered confidence, sister.

Some years ago I came across what became the most life-changing, transformative tool ever called *The Work* by author and teacher, Byron Katie.[3]

Katie, as people call her, says: "A thought is harmless unless we believe it. It's not our thoughts, but our attachment to our thoughts, that causes suffering. Attaching to a thought means believing that it's true, without inquiring. And a belief is a thought that we've been attaching to, often for years."

I mean, boom.

Right? RIGHT?!

It's our *attachment* to our thoughts that causes suffering. It's not the thoughts themselves – thoughts are just thoughts. It's how we react to them that causes our own suffering.

Byron Katie has written a game-changing book (it's the book I have gifted the most in my life) called *Loving What Is: Four Questions That Can Change Your Life* and I couldn't recommend any stronger that you get your hands on it. She is an absolute expert when it comes to self-inquiry.

She is incredibly generous and offers a ton of worksheets, articles and resources for free, so make sure you Google her and get into her amazing content. Even if you put this book down right now so you can search her real quick, I would actually be okay with that – she has changed my freaking life.

Byron Katie is literally changing the world with her work, because managing your mind and inquiring your thoughts is the key to EVERYTHING you want.

When you investigate your thoughts, you strip them down and have the ability to find what's *really* true. And it's only when you pull the thought apart, that you see it's just a stress inducing *story* you've been telling yourself that is not serving you – and that only when you believe it do you suffer.

If you inquire, you could end your own suffering. (No big deal, right?)

She talks about loving "what is" instead of fighting with what is. Instead of fighting with your reality, learn to love it, learn to be at peace and be free from the story.

In a short summary below is Byron's Katie's four question process (please promise me you'll get her book because there is SO much more depth to this and it will actually blow your mind).

You start by thinking *one specific thought* that has been bringing you stress lately, and then inquire with the four questions and finish with the "turnaround."

Question one – Is it true?

(This is about you closing your eyes and really going within yourself to see if what you are thinking is true, a yes or no answer.)

Question two – Can you absolutely know that it's true?

(Again, an invitation for you to see if the thought you are thinking is actually true, a yes or no answer.)

Question three – How do you react, what happens, when you believe that thought?

(When you believe the thought, how do you live, who do you become, what do you do, what emotions come up, what is your action, reaction, inaction etc.)

Question four – Who would you be without that thought?

(If you actually could erase the thought from your mind, if it didn't exist – how would you live? Who would you be?)

Then the Turnaround, where she encourages you to turn that thought around in three different ways, in order to find a thought that is truer than the original stressful thought.

Let me share with you just one of my many examples on how this work helped me in my life…

SO…my husband is not a romantic guy.

He's just not, and I'm a super romantic, thoughtful person – hello, my love languages are words of affirmation and physical touch! My husband Hamish on the other hand was just never the "romantic" type.

When I first discovered Byron Katie and *The Work* I did the four questions on this (extremely frustrating and stressful) thought, and here's what I wrote in my journal:

Hamish is not romantic.

Is it true?

I began writing really fast and messy. "Um, yeah it's true! I don't see any flower deliveries happening?! I mean, he never gets me flowers, he's not thoughtful at all, he doesn't sweep me off my feet or look me in the eyes and tell me how beautiful I am EVER! SO YEAH, HE IS NOT ROMANTIC, he's actually so freaking rude and he's SELFISH!"

Can you absolutely know that it's true?

(Ah Byron Katie, she gets me every time on question two!)

"Well? Um…yeah? I think so…hmmm…ugh, I don't know? There was that one time he bought me flowers on Valentine's day – like three years ago?…Can I know for sure? Okay, a yes or no answer… hmmm…"

Now, I was so angry at the time that I forgot the most important part of her work of inquiry, which is to close your eyes and do it like a mediation. See the person in your mind, see them acting out your stressful thought, is it true? Is that really true?

So I closed my eyes…

I see my husband doing the daily things.

I see him waking up early so I can have a sleep in (most mornings), I see him getting the kids ready, making them breakfast, grabbing me a coffee, cleaning the whole house, washing my car…

When I actually tuned in to all the things he was doing, I had to say, "No, I can't know for sure. Could this be *his* idea of "romance"? I mean, it wasn't flowers and compliments but he actually is an incredible man and he does do so much for me."

After answering question two I realized that my original thought, "Hamish is not romantic," was actually a stressful, untrue story (at the time my mind was blown).

How do you react, what happens, when you believe that thought (or in my case, the story)?

This one was hard to write and actually where more epiphanies happened…

"I become angry and passive aggressive, I get stand-offish, I think he's an inconsiderate asshole, I treat him like shit, I am cold to him, I tell him he's not thoughtful and that he's not romantic...I treat him brashly, I disengage and have a little bubble of resentment and give him the silent treatment..."

WHOA. What the fuck?!

When I believe the bullshit story, I actually treat him like shit and I become an asshole, and I'm not romantic to HIM. This was all starting to make sense. No wonder he didn't want to buy me flowers!

I expect him to be romantic to ME when I'm being so rude to him? When I'm demanding to be loved and adored by slamming doors and having a grown ass temper tantrum?

I was actually being hard to love, and I was pushing my husband away when I was believing that thought. Since I didn't inquire, I actually took that thought, ran with it, made it the truth and decided to make that *my* reality. I became the *thought in action*.

THIS is the danger of not inquiring – you start to believe the bullshit you're telling yourself, you then act it out and get the result of it. Question three becomes your state of being, so when you encounter other people, how you live and how you react is who THEY react to. It's a hot mess!

I was actually creating this angry husband because I was being angry and rude to him, so of course he didn't want to buy me any flowers!

Who would you be without the thought?

Okay, so if I could NEVER have that thought, who would I be?

"I'd be happy, fulfilled, I'd appreciate my husband...I would focus on all the things he's doing for me, rather than the stuff he's NOT doing. I'd be nice to him, I'd probably be happier...

he'd be happier, we'd be happier! I would tell him how much he means to me, and I would probably notice how much he DOES do around the house. WOW."

When I focus on the fact that he's **not** romantic, that's all I can see. And what does "romantic" actually mean? According to me, flowers and telling me I'm pretty. For Hamish, cleaning the whole house is his romantic gesture!

SINCE I DIDN'T INQUIRE, I ACTUALLY TOOK THAT THOUGHT, RAN WITH IT, MADE IT THE TRUTH AND DECIDED TO MAKE THAT MY REALITY.

Then there is the Turnaround – this is extremely tricky but it's where the biggest breakthroughs happen. Once you read or listen to her book enough times you'll get it, it takes practice.

You take the initial thought: *"Hamish is not romantic"* and you do the three turnarounds.

Turnaround to the self: *"I'm not romantic to myself."* This was so damn true. I can love myself, I can buy myself flowers, I can tell myself I'm pretty! I'm expecting him to do something I clearly want, but I don't even do it for myself?!

Turnaround to the other: *"I am not romantic to Hamish."* Ouch, this was also true. I'm telling him "you're not romantic, you're so selfish, you're not thoughtful…" meanwhile I am thinking he's being an asshole when really, I'm not being nice to him, so why would he want to be romantic to me when I'm showcasing that behavior?!

Turnaround to the opposite: *"My husband is romantic."* Also true, as acts of service are clearly the way he expresses romance – by showing me he cares instead of telling me.

Byron Katie says that as long as you can find one out of the three turnarounds that is more truthful than the original thought (all three were true in my example), then you're on the right track.

(Also a little update – my husband is super romantic these days! He buys flowers and does all the beautiful thoughtful stuff all the time…why? Because I too am romantic to him, and to myself.)

Since I used to frame him as this selfish man who wasn't romantic, that's all I could ever see. I was focusing on what he WASN'T, instead of realizing ALL that he was. I shifted my focus, changed my thoughts, changed my feelings and behavior towards him, and I CHANGED. MY. REALITY. It changed our entire relationship.

If you let go of the guilt and the anxiety and focus on inquiry – what is really true, what's not, and who do you become when you believe it versus who you are without it – you can create clarity about what's really going on, and then take steps towards letting go of the stressful stories that would normally run your life for years on end.

This work frees you and when you're no longer a prisoner of your mind, you become unlimited, you become free from the suffering and you are able to CREATE a mindset that continues to serve you and others moving forward. 👑

CHAPTER 4

#FWOT

I'm a loud sneezer. Like, really loud.

When I sneeze it's going at 900mph – it sounds like a flying missile and there is nothing pretty, "lady like" or elegant about it, whatsoever.

I've always been a loud sneezer (and so is my mom) and the first time I knew it was "different" was at school, because all the kids in school would jump out of their seats every time I sneezed during a test.

But until my late 20s, I didn't realize I was an *offensive* sneezer. Yup, apparently my big ol' sneeze offended people, in a really big way. Let me explain…

So, after my first Australian boyfriend didn't work out, I met another guy…and un-luckily for me, this guy was just like the last guy, only a little nicer and a little more of a people pleaser. When we started dating, I felt so utterly inferior to him in every way possible. I attracted him shortly after breaking up with Aussie guy #1 – let's call him Narcissist Ned. Eight months after we broke up I met Aussie guy #2, People Pleasing Peter. (Note: the names of these a-holes have been changed in order to protect the not-so-innocent.)

When we're hanging at my apartment and he hears me sneeze, he doesn't say anything. But if we were in public, he would look at me and ask me: "Is that really how you sneeze?! Why do you sneeze so loud?" He was offended. Outraged! For a woman and her sneeze to create that much noise and take up that much space.

I thought, what a weird question? Of course that's how I sneeze. But I moved on.

A little while later we were at his family's house and I sneezed again. The whole family looked at me in shock and horror. They seemed genuinely offended. That's when I put two and two together: ah, this is why he hates my sneezes! His family doesn't approve.

Holy shit. Something's wrong with me. I am not good enough. This family does not like me. At all...

They don't like me! They don't like my loud mouth, they especially don't like my loud sneezes and I am not good enough for these people or their son!

So what did I do?

I stopped giving a fuck what other people thought about my God damn sneezes, I kept sneezing loud as hell, dumped his wack-ass and moved on with my life.

Ha! I wish...

That's what the Erika of today would do. Erika back then was a totally different person.

You see, he and his family were completely obsessed with caring about what other people thought of them. They were super judgmental and it was so ingrained in them to care what people think, that even my loud sneeze knocked their socks off. (Picture the mother whispering to her husband: "We can't take her to a family get together with that sneeze, can we?!")

And what I did was textbook #lowselfworth.

I held in my sneezes. (Thankfully, this was before childbirth and good old incontinence kicked in! Can you imagine?)

I don't actually know how I did that? I had all these sneezes that went un-sneezed; I wonder what happened to them?

All I knew was that my boyfriend and his family did not like my sneezes – they were openly offended by them – so I started holding them in.

Because it was all gonna be okay, as long as they liked me right?

How that particular little experience manifested in my mind was: my sneezes are loud, offensive and awful, therefore I am loud, offensive and awful. My sneezes are just another reason why I'm not sophisticated enough or educated enough or good enough.

Good girls don't sneeze like that. What is wrong with me?!

And the sneeze was just the cherry on top – this guy had asked me to lie to his family about everything about my past and my history, and basically delete who I was. (Yeah, there were no wedding bells ringing for us.)

WHAT OTHER PEOPLE

think of me is none of my business.

— WAYNE DYER —

LIVING A LIE

Let me be one hundred percent clear when I say: it was my own stuff that was getting triggered by them. If someone had a problem with my sneeze today, I'd laugh and not give them an ounce of my energy. You don't like my sneeze? That's your problem, not mine.

But at the time I had no self-worth, no confidence and really lacked self-belief – so my own inner demons were brought out by their insecurities and projections. It was like their judgment was shining a massive spotlight on me and everything that was "wrong" with me. Girl, I wish I had known about #FWOT back then. The amount of time, energy and fucks I wasted…

Unfortunately I wasn't a FWOT Queen back in those days. So, here's what really happened: I stopped sneezing around them. I fixed that "flaw" (at great personal discomfort) and did they start accepting me and loving me from that point on?

Of course not – they found something else they didn't like about me.

And something else. And something else…

And no matter what I did, it wasn't good enough for them.

Therefore I felt: "I'm not a good enough person."

Honestly, I could have worn matching sweater sets and immaculate makeup and been careful, sweet, kind and walked on eggshells and they would keep changing the goal posts on me. They changed the goal posts because they had decided I wasn't enough for their son or their family – so they were going to do and say whatever they wanted to confirm that. The end result was me living a lie for the 11 months that we were together.

The sneezes were just the tip of the iceberg: he also couldn't bear his parents knowing that I came from a broken family, so he lied and told his family that my parents were still together but having issues. He wouldn't tell them my "shameful" past as a bikini model or that I had been married prior to meeting him, or that I had experienced a lot of painful trauma in my past.

Shit – he wouldn't even tell them about our (secret) trip overseas together. I mean come on dude, you're 30 years old, tell your mother the truth!

I kept up with his charade until it got really painful; until I had no more energy left to pretend. I finally realized I wasn't being true to me, and I was chasing my tail trying to impress people who (I now realize) lacked so much confidence and self worth themselves.

I had realized that coming to Australia to run away from my past wasn't working.

I had finally realized that I had lost all my confidence.

I had allowed myself to feel so insignificant in that relationship that I lost all sense who I really was.

But most importantly – I had realized that saying yes to please others was a big no to myself. I vowed to start mending the relationship I had lacked with myself.

It was the moment I finally gave up trying to impress other people.

WHY DO WE GIVE SO MANY FUCKS?

Have you ever thought about WHY women lack confidence?

Why women struggle to take up space, speak our truth and own who we are, as we are?

This was something that consumed my mind when I first started my coaching business.

I read books on it, I jumped into forums about it, I read studies, stats and papers galore.

And I asked every single woman I came into contact with the same question: "Why do you think you lack confidence?"

Over the years I would get a variety of answers, but they ALL led me back to one common denominator: we give too many fucks about what people think of us.

We allow the opinion of others to prevent us from showing up.

And we care way too much about being liked, fitting in and playing it safe.

During my time as a stylist I found some disturbing stats to back my research on why women cared so much about the opinion of others.

In 2016, the Dove Global Beauty and Confidence report interviewed 10,500 women across 13 countries and it showed some shocking statistics when it comes to how women and girls view themselves.

The research showed that eighty-five percent of women will opt out or cancel important life activities like hanging out with friends and loved ones, or going to a job interview or a social function, when they don't feel good about their image and the way they see themselves.[4]

This results in approximately eight out of ten women choosing to opt out of their lives because they care too much about what others have to say!

That's not all. Dove's research also shows that fifty-six percent of women are acutely feeling the pressure to be "perfect" because of the impact of social media. Nearly eight in ten (seventy-eight percent) of women and girls report feeling some pressure to never make mistakes or show weakness.

Ummmm…Who said we should never make mistakes or show weakness? Excuse me?! WHAT?!

The amount of pressure we put on ourselves to "get it right" and be perceived as perfect is just not sustainable.

Is this the message we share with our kids: "Unless you can do it perfectly, don't bother trying at all"? Hell no!

> ## FIFTY-SIX PERCENT OF WOMEN ARE ACUTELY FEELING THE PRESSURE TO BE "PERFECT" BECAUSE OF THE IMPACT OF SOCIAL MEDIA.

No wonder why so many of us blame social media as the reason why we don't feel good enough!

By the way – social media cannot "make" you lack confidence. It's a tool that we use (most of us ineffectively.) Blaming the gram for why you're not confident is not going to help.

Loving bitch-slap alert: you don't have to follow those horrible accounts.

You know the ones, I don't have to spell it out for you – they're the ones who's posts almost always lead you to comparing yourself and then feeling like shit for the rest of the day.

You have a choice in the matter. Why not CHOOSE to unfollow all of those accounts that **you know** are no good for you?

This is a perfect time and place to take your response – ability back.

On the flip side, the study also showed that seven out of ten women reported feeling more confident or positive when they invested time in caring for themselves.

Self care, growth, boundaries and you doing you – this is the way you overcome the social media blame game. I can't tell you how many women I've met and worked with over the years, who have spent their ENTIRE lives worried about what other people think of them.

And for a very long time, I was one of those women.

Believe it or not, caring what people think of you is actually a pretty common thing humans do and it's perfectly normal. Where it becomes a big problem is when you allow the opinion of others to *stop you* from going for what you want in life – that's different.

One is a *stock-standard* (subconscious) way to live – most of us still care what other people think of us at some level (you can thank our 200-million-year-old brain for that, hello tribe mentality and the need to fit in).

The other will actually *rob you of your happiness.*

It's human nature to want to fit in and be liked. Back in the days of our prehistoric ancestors, our lives literally depended on it. Living in a tribe became a basic survival skill and if your tribe rejected you, it could mean being exiled from the community, which led to death.

In those days we literally had to avoid rejection to stay alive.

This is one of the reasons we struggle with fitting in and being liked today: being accepted by our tribe was actually the key to our survival.

Now, that made total sense way back then when you had some serious wildlife hanging around just waiting to eat you. But in today's world, rejection won't get you eaten by a tiger. Instead, you'll most likely just fall flat on your ass publicly and you'll be embarrassed – but being embarrassed won't kill you.

And with approximately eight billion people on the planet today, trust me when I tell you that they are not all your people. They're not all going to like you (hell, you don't like everyone you meet!). You will get rejected, that's guaranteed. So you have to learn to live with that.

You've gotta find your people, find your circle. But how do we do this when we're constantly trying to fit in and be liked, when we're people pleasing, being perfectionists or worse, a "recovering perfectionist" (can we please just stop calling ourselves that already?)

Or when we're comparing ourselves, shape shifting and pretending to be a certain way just so that "they" like you?

This is why you need to embody #FWOT – ASAP sister.

FWOT is not about "Fuck those people" vibes. It's about "fuck that!" It's the energy of "Who cares what they think? I am going to do me – regardless."

It recognizes that you may care about what other people think or say about you, but you will not allow that to stop you from living your life and going for your dreams and desires.

This is another one of those important concepts you need to own when you start creating confidence. It's actually the key to gaining momentum while you're in the practice of confidence.

HOW TO ACTUALLY STOP GIVING A FUCK

After years (or even decades) of people pleasing and living according to other people's expectations, and being consumed by anxiety about how others judge you...how do you make this change?

How can you just accept that the opinion of others *truly doesn't matter* and continue doing what you're doing, without letting what they think of you impact the way you see yourself?

You can start by accepting that people can be, often are, and will continue to be wrong **about you**.

Say it with me now:

I will let people be wrong about me.

People WILL be wrong about me.

And I will let them be.

Here's the thing: people WILL be wrong about you – all the time!

They will think whatever they want to think about you NO MATTER what you do. People will form opinions about you that aren't accurate.

They'll have something to say, whether you're too shy or too loud, you're too skinny, or too curvy, you're too ambitious, you're not driven enough...the list goes on.

The question for you is, instead of worrying about that noise, can you let them be wrong about you?

Can you stop yourself from constantly needing to correct, defend or argue with people who have ALREADY made up their minds about who **they think** you are?

You saw in my example with Mr. Anti-sneezes – it didn't matter if I shape-shifted into Princess Jasmine herself, that family was not going to like me. That guy was never, ever going to think I was good enough!

I know it's not easy to just "let them be wrong about you" but you must realize that you actually have no choice as to how other people decide to perceive you (remember? It's out of your control).

So instead of fighting this, decide right now that it won't impact you. Tell yourself they will be wrong – and let them be.

This means you don't give those people attention. And you definitely don't ask them for **their** opinion on **your** life.

You draw some serious boundaries on who you let into your life and who you're willing to take advice from.

It will feel so hard in the beginning, but if you don't commit to starting this new way of thinking now it will only get harder. If you continue to allow other people's opinions to run your life (as I was doing in my relationship with the sneeze hater) then you'll be teaching these people how to treat you.

What you allow will continue; if I didn't decide to change my behavior, I would've ended up attracting yet another relationship just like the ones I'd had before.

ANYTHING THAT STARTS WITH "I DON'T WANT THEM TO THINK..." WILL END IN YOU NOT STANDING AS YOUR FULLY EXPRESSED SELF.

ERIKA CRAMER

START TRUSTING YOURSELF

This is one of the many ways you'll learn how to #FWOT. Instead of going outwards for advice or ideas on what to do next, learn to trust yourself. Give yourself the chance to decide what's best for you. (Even if it's wrong, that's okay – you gotta start somewhere!)

Start getting better at silencing the external "noise" and start listening to your internal voice. You and every other woman in the world has everything she needs inside of her. I know it sounds like some bullshit Instagram quote, but it's true. The problem is that we don't believe it.

So, we go outside of ourselves and we ask others what they think we should do, way too often.

We listen to our judgmental cousin about what we should do in our career, even though homegirl has been unemployed or in an out of jobs since high school. We ask our broke-ass friends about financial decisions we want to make, and we seek the advice of our parents when wanting to start a new business, when they see entrepreneurship as risky and irresponsible.

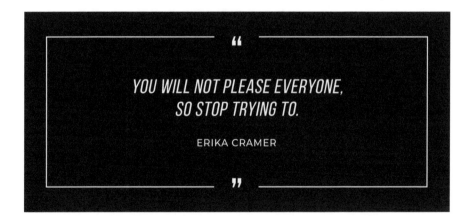

> YOU WILL NOT PLEASE EVERYONE, SO STOP TRYING TO.
>
> ERIKA CRAMER

The more we do this, the quieter our internal voice becomes. No wonder we are seeking to be validated, to be liked and to be told what we should do instead of going for what WE want.

Maybe your internal voice is a whisper right now and if that's the case, you need to listen and trust yourself even more.

Here's a little exercise I give my clients who need to make a decision about something important, but they are unsure what to do...

» Go somewhere quiet, where you can have some privacy and ideally not be interrupted.

» Have a pen and paper nearby.

» Close down your eyes and put one hand on your heart and the other hand on your stomach.

» Take five to ten really slow, deep breaths. Be very mindful, intentional and present.

» Think of the decision you need to make, and visualize what outcome you are hoping for. What is it that you'd love to happen?

» Tune into your stomach or G.U.T. (Give Up Thinking) as Wayne Dyer calls it.

» Get out of your head and get into your body.

» Pay attention...

» How do you feel about this decision?

» Does it feel good?

» Are you nervous but a little excited?

» Or do you feel fearful and anxious?

» Does it feel like something's not right?

» Open your eyes when you have your feelings and write them out on paper – sometimes if I'm really torn, I make a list of the pros and the cons. Let yourself write how you feel and what you want to do. Most importantly, you want to make sure you tap into the feeling.

» That is your intuition, your internal voice.

The way I differentiate between FEAR and INTUITION is by paying attention to how I feel.

If I have a bunch of irrational, negative, fearful thoughts (stories) racing around in my mind, then I know I'm in fear.

When I close my eyes, check in with my FEELING and get into my body – that's my intuition.

My fear is usually future-focused. It feels like anxiety and it happens when I am living in my head; there are usually a bunch of scary sentences running through my mind (and many of them start with "what if this worst-case scenario happens?").

If you are always asking other people what they think you should do, you'll need to practice this exercise regularly. It's simple yet extremely powerful.

Because the reality is, you wont get your answer when you're constantly asking others for theirs.

STOP TRYING TO CONVERT THE CRITICS

Another powerful way to embrace the #FWOT way of life is to learn how to embrace the critics.

Yes, you read that right. Why?

Think about it: what do critics do? They criticize, right? As they say, "haters are gonna hate." So why would you expect anything different from them?

People who are criticizing you do **not** get to have your attention, unless you willingly give it to them.

While writing this book, I imagined people disagreeing with me. Imagined readers not liking the book: how much I swore, or how much pink there is, or the advice I was sharing, or the kind of font I chose…the list goes on.

And you know what, there is no way in the world that this book (or I) will ever please everyone.

The reality is that there are people who will think my book is shit and they won't like it and that's OKAY!

They're clearly not my people! Simple.

So instead of trying to perfect my book and make it consumable for everyone (that one size fits all bullshit – no thank you) I'm doing me! I'll write in the same tone as I speak, and with the same bold ass, pink, analogy loving, cheetah print-flavor I weave into everything else I do.

Because it's MY book.

When I try to please those who quite literally are unpleasable – I change who I am and what I am about. When I start changing who I am, what I stand for and how I show up, it turns me into someone I am not. Then I have not only confused "my people, my circle, my readers and supporters," but I have confused myself as well.

I will never convert my critics or make someone like me and I am okay with that.

I invite you to become okay with that, too.

PERFECTIONISM WILL KILL YOUR CONFIDENCE

Perfection and judgment are like your evil cousins. When you are trying to be perfect (which I know *you know* is impossible) you become extremely judgmental.

The two go hand in hand and they also tend to hang out with our friend comparison as well – they are a detrimental trio. Here's how it looks:

Perfectionism leads you to being unnecessarily hard on yourself (and others).

The judgment kicks in when you feel that you haven't done it the best way possible (let's be honest, everything can always improve, nothing will ever be perfect).

Therefore you tend to also judge others for their efforts and where they may fall short.

And/or, you compare yourself to others who you *think* are perfect and who you think "have it all together," which once again makes you judge yourself and judge them…

Can you see this vicious cycle at play?

When you're seeking perfectionism, you're most likely scared.

Scared to be seen, scared to be criticized and scared to get it wrong.

When you're busy trying to be perfect, you don't allow yourself to learn from your mistakes and this impacts your ability to create confidence.

If you are a perfectionist, you'll have to come to terms with the fact that you are not and never ever will be perfect. No one is.

You'll have to come to terms with the fact that you will fuck shit up, royally, multiple times in your life until you learn how to do it better.

Lastly, if you're a parent this loving bitch-slap is for you: PLEASE commit to working on this "perfectionist" bullshit. Even if you think you're not handing this perceived pressure onto your children, you most likely are.

Remember, our kids don't listen to what we say, they pay attention to what we DO.

Here's another loving bitch-slap for you – you're judgmental. I am too. We all are.

Let's not sugar-coat it. Studies show that we judge a person within 100 milliseconds of meeting them.[5] Again, if you find yourself **constantly** picking yourself apart and judging yourself harshly on the daily, then you become SUPER judgmental of others.

I have a theory that when you're constantly looking for the negative in yourself, then you can't help but look for the "negative" in others.

Let's say you look in the mirror and start criticizing the wrinkles around your eyes. You start to hone in on this in other women. You better believe that when you see a woman with crows feet or deep smile lines walking by you, you are most likely judging that woman as well (or comparing yourself).

When all we do is tear ourselves apart, how can we expect to see the goodness in others?

As you tear yourself apart, you train your eyes to do this subconsciously in others.

For me personally, I used to hate public speaking – HATE it! And I'm not alone: did you know that the fear of public speaking is the most common phobia ahead of death? As the incredible Jerry Seinfeld says:

"At a funeral, most people would rather be the guy in the coffin than have to stand up and give a eulogy."[6]

The American National Institute of Mental Health even reports that public speaking anxiety (or glossophobia as it's called) affects about seventy-three percent of the population.[7]

The underlying fear here is "judgment and negative evaluation by others," which translates to – we again are fearful of what other people think of us! If that doesn't fuel the fact that we care too much what others think, then what will?!

In the past, whenever I had to speak in public, I would get really tense, my hands would start sweating and I would feel the flush of anxiety run through my body, so much so that the heat would make my cheeks red. It was horrifying.

And guess what I discovered? Every time I went to see someone speak at a wedding, a social function or a work event, I would judge the shit out of the speakers…not on purpose or consciously, but I would do it!

Lets keep it real: we judge. You judge! I judge! It happens!

But I'd find myself at an event or function and I would be picking the speaker apart. "Oh, I don't like what she's wearing…

Yeah, she was okay, but I didn't find her that funny…She speaks too fast/too slow/too high/too low…"

I was as **JUDGMENTAL AF!**

No wonder when the day came for me to stand on stage and speak I was shitting myself. Helloooo! I had judged other speakers so much that naturally, when I stepped on that stage I thought everyone in the audience was going to be judging me the same way.

Now, I obviously had NO idea that this was happening at the time – it wasn't until doing this work and learning about my insecure projections that I realized how I was behaving.

The day I decided to stop being an asshole to myself, I stopped doing it to others. As a matter of fact, I stopped allowing others to judge and gossip negatively in front of me as well. This toxic habit only breeds more negativity and judgment into your life.

The great poet, memoirist, and civil rights activist Maya Angelou says this on the topic of gossip: "I'm convinced that the negative has power – and if you allow it to perch in your house, in your mind, in your life, it can take you over."

She also says: "Those negative words climb into the woodwork, into the furniture, and the next thing you know, they're on your skin. A negative statement is poison."[8]

The beauty of FWOT is, it has different levels.

The first is letting go of the opinion of others, but the deeper level is actually realizing that other people's opinions are not a reflection of you – but a deep seeded insecurity they hold, mixed with a lack of responsibility and their own low self-belief. The truth is, it never has anything to do with you; it was always their stuff.

And when you really master this concept, not only do you gain the freedom to "do you," but you actually gain a whole new level of compassion for those who are so deeply judgmental. You wish for them that one day they too get to see how amazing they are and that the power never lies in criticizing others – it lies in uplifting others.

BE KIND, SAY NO: WORD TO MY PEOPLE PLEASERS

I want you to consider these questions and see whether any of these are an issue for you…

- Do you find yourself constantly comparing yourself to other women?

- Would you say you're a perfectionist or a "recovering perfectionist"? (It's the same thing, by the way.)

- Do you say yes when you really want to say no?

- If so, do you say yes because are you worried about sounding or being mean?

- Do you find yourself shrinking or playing small so you don't get noticed?

- When someone doesn't like you, how does it affect you?

- Are you always trying to "get it right"?

Last question: have you ever considered why you do this?

Are you starting to understand why I keep telling you to let "them" be wrong about you?

If you can't handle the idea that someone else doesn't like you or something you've said or done, then this is an area I invite you to go deeper into.

I said it before and I am going to say it again sister: people WILL be wrong about you.

They will make assumptions, they will judge you, they will try and put you in a box so that they can feel better about their judgment. They won't like something you say, something you wear, how you act, the decisions you make.

And you don't need to let ANY OF THAT impact you.

I once had a client who was a mother of three kids aged under six. She was a stay-at-home mom and she was always busy with the kids, she didn't get much sleep since one of her kids was co-sleeping. She was exhausted from constantly cooking and cleaning up after them.

The only person you **NEED TO SEEK APPROVAL FROM,** *is you*

— ERIKA CRAMER —

Her sister had two kids around the same age as her youngest. Her sister dealt with motherhood differently and she'd get really stressed out from time to time, so she'd call on my client with an SOS: "Can you babysit the kids this weekend? I need a break…"

My client had a beautiful, calm, mothering vibe and she knew her sister was struggling. She wanted to be helpful, so she'd say yes.

She'd then have five kids in her home under the age of six (OMG I'd run) and she started to feel the pressure.

Before long, her sister started dropping the kids off regularly as my client had all of a sudden become her "go-to" babysitter.

My client didn't say no. She'd put on her fake smile and take the kids, because she didn't want to say no or be mean to her sister, right?

So what happened? She became resentful that she was stuck with extra kids to look after all the time. This in turn made her short and snappy with her kids and her husband. Once her sister's kids would leave, she would be extremely over-tired and not interested in cooking or cleaning or being present with her husband.

When he'd dare to ask what was wrong, the truth came out…

"I just can't believe her! Doesn't she know how tired I am?! I mean, we have three kids ourselves, it's not like I sit here at home all day doing nothing, then she shows up AGAIN asking me to babysit – doesn't she know how unfair it is for her to keep dropping the kids here?! I mean seriously, she's such an inconsiderate bitch! Doesn't she know?!"

No. She doesn't "know."

Because my client NEVER TOLD HER. Ever.

Her sister thinks my client LOVES babysitting her kids! Why?

Because she always says yes, never complains, is smiling and happy to take them and has never once communicated that she's unhappy with the situation.

See what actually happens when we try to be "nice" by saying yes? We can end up becoming manipulative, resentful and angry, we end up bitching and gossiping behind the back of the person we're trying to please…and in fact – that's not so "nice" of us, is it?

We're so worried about being "mean" or disappointing someone else by saying no – when in reality, we actually become mean and disappointing in other passive aggressive, gossiping ways (and we end up taking it out on other people, usually the people we love who have nothing to do with our people pleasing bullshit.)

So how do you move from a place of "OMG they don't like me" or "I can't disappoint them" to "I'm moving forward with this and I don't care what you think about it?"

You can start with this exercise – if you are a people pleaser, this is gonna be fun.

I want you to think of someone you say yes to (someone you "please") when in reality you want to say no.

Imagine yourself saying NO to them. Some ideas to get you thinking: it might be the school mom friend who asks you to look after her kids; the friend who asks to borrow your car on the regular; the co-worker that asks you to cover for them "just this once" (again)…you get my drift.

I want you to imagine yourself saying "no" to them. And then ask yourself: And then what will happen?

In my client's example:

My sister asks me to babysit her kids for the night, again. I say no.

And then what? *My sister gets mad at me.*

And then what? *She yells at me, tells me I'm being rude and inconsiderate and gives me the silent treatment.*

And then what? *She doesn't talk to me for a week and starts bitching to other family members about me.*

And then what? *She calls me again in three days and tells me how angry she is.*

And then what? And then what? And then what?

Seriously, what's the worst that can happen?

People will get over it eventually.

They will process **THEIR** shit and you get to release the control of how they decide to feel. If they don't get over it – that's not your problem. You can decide to move on. The worst-case scenario is your sister thinks you're a bitch (well now you're even!) but did you die though?

EVEN BETTER: when you go through this process of setting boundaries with people and saying what you actually mean (in this case, no instead of yes) you start to teach people how to treat you. (Read that last line again please.)

That's the best part about all this.

In every interaction you have, you are teaching people how to treat you.

When you constantly put others' needs before your own, say yes, when you mean no – they start to expect that from you.

It's called putting you first: what do you need?

Ask yourself this and be prepared to give it to yourself **BEFORE** you give to anyone else.

And if you have already been teaching people how to treat you (in the negative ways) guess what?

You can RE-teach them how to treat you!

It's up to you to stand up for yourself and create the healthy boundaries you need to be happy and fulfilled.

It's not too late for that.

BE KIND, SAY NO.

— ERIKA CRAMER —

JUST BE LIKE ELSA AND LET IT GO, YO!

– ERIKA CRAMER –

Let's talk about the importance of surrendering.

At some point, you will crack; my cracking point was 11 months of holding my sneezes in. What's yours going to be?

At the end of the day, you can't put on this charade for too long – you will eventually get sick and tired of pretending.

If you speak to anyone over 70 years old, they will tell you they don't give a damn what anyone has to say about them anymore. I once spoke to a woman at an aged care home and her biggest regret was not doing what SHE wanted and always trying to please everyone else around her.

Surrender.

It requires you not trying.

It requires you trusting that the path of least resistance is the way through.

The more "you" you become, the more your people will find you.

WHAT IS IT COSTING YOU?

Who would you be without your disempowering story?

I really want you to think about this.

Sit with it for a minute.

By now you most likely know what your disempowering story is already: it's the reason why you're feeling "stuck" or in a lack. And for many of us, it's rooted in what other people say and think about us.

So, I want to end this chapter asking you this:

Who could you be if you didn't allow the opinion of others to mess with you on the daily?

Have you ever thought of what it's actually costing you to live your life constantly worrying about the opinion of others?

Have you ever thought about what it's COSTING you to let the opinion of others stop you from living?

When you care too much about what other people think about you it's costing you.

A lot. And it's also costing your family, your children, your friends, your co-workers…it's actually costing the world.

You may have never thought about it like this but you must.

In your career: you stay in the crappy, safe job because it's familiar and it's what you know and it's secure. But it's not what you're passionate about (you're actually really interested in something totally different – let's say, the environment and sustainability).

You stay in that job, miserably half-assing your work and going through the motions.

You do this instead of actually living your passion and changing the world when it comes to educating others on sustainability…

THE COST:

— Your fulfillment

— Your happiness

— Your passion

— Your purpose

— Your ability to change the world

— Your financial freedom

— Your capacity to contribute.

In your relationships, the cost could be even higher. Some of you reading along right now *know you* should be divorced – you know that your marriage or partnership is costing you your happiness, your dignity and your spirit. And what is it costing your kids?

It could be showing them a flawed and fucked up model for "love." It could be costing them the chance of having a happy and present mom in their life.

THE COST:

- Your happiness

- Finding true love

- Being present and honest with your children

- Being a role model for what love looks like to your children

- Your truth

- Your desires

- Your sex and intimacy

- Your passion

In your life, you've always doubted yourself therefore you don't take any risks. You get opportunities all the time but you live in fear so instead of following your heart and soul you stay where you are – miserable and unhappy, wishing things could be different.

THE COST:

- Your happiness

- Your joy

- Your freedom

- Excitement

- Fun and spontaneity

- Adventure

The cost is MASSIVE! It costs you and it costs others A LOT!

I know, these things are hard to read, but I want you to really and truly look at what your choices are costing you and the people you love.

I want you to imagine what your life could look like if you actually went for what you wanted – what would you bring to the world? In what ways could you light a spark, serve, deliver and make a real impact?

It reminds me of the words by the incredible author, spiritual leader, politician and activist Marianne Williamson. You may have read her poem "Our Deepest Fear"[9] before – but ever since I discovered it, it changed my life forever. If you haven't read it yet please go google it now!

It is your light that scares you most?

What does it cost you to play small and not stand in your power?

What does it cost your children when you don't believe in yourself? What does it cost your clients when you don't take up space or show up?

What legacy do you get to leave if you are too busy giving too many fucks about what other people are thinking of you?

What does it cost the world, if you're here to make an impact and somehow make the world a better place – but you're too stuck in worrying about "what people think" to go for it?

I'm not saying you have to be Oprah and leave a massive legacy for the world. But whatever you came here to do on this planet, won't happen if you keep living like this.

The bottom line is when you're pretending to be someone you're not just so people can like you – you suffer.

So if you didn't have any fear of what others may think of you, who would you be? What would you do?

Letting people be wrong about you is not easy, but once you do, you gain freedom, you gain self-belief, you learn to trust yourself and have your own back for once.

You learn how to fill your own cup without ever needing anyone else to "make you whole" or validate you, because you end up doing that for yourself, which makes practicing confidence so much easier.

The reality is: no one knows who you are sister. I mean, you're still discovering who you are – so how can someone outside of you know you, when you're still learning about yourself? We all are.

I know that the opinion of others can't define me, because I am a work in progress and I am constantly evolving and changing.

And so are you. 👑

CHAPTER 5

CONFIDENCE
AS A
practice

The woman **who does not require validation** from anyone is the **most feared individual on the planet.**

— MOHADESA NAJUMI —

By now you're probably starting to realize that being confident is not at all what you thought it would be, huh?

Confidence isn't a beautiful woman with shiny red lips and stilettos, stalking across the room with all eyes on her.

In fact, to be confident, you don't have to be good-looking, extroverted, bold, loud, outgoing, polished or someone who likes to be the center of the attention.

That's not what confidence is.

True confidence is when you feel the fear, the anxiety, the unfamiliarity or strangeness of a situation or experience – and you step into it anyway.

You move forward. You try it. You give it a go. You experiment.

You move forward knowing that if you try something, you fall flat on your face and it doesn't work out, then, so what? You can pick yourself up and try again. You actually have to if you're ever going to create confidence.

Reaching this place where you can "feel the fear and do it anyway" is the real premise of the work I do around confidence. And what I really want you to know is that this is not a "destination," or place to "get to."

It's ongoing work, which is why I call it the "practice" of confidence.

I've briefly mentioned throughout the book the idea that confidence is a practice, and I want to explain why I think of it like that.

Have you ever tried meditating?

I suck at it. Like, really badly.

And my husband Hamish is a meditation teacher (ironic, huh?).

I should be so good at it, shouldn't I? I have an amazing teacher by my side. But I'm not. Why? Because I never practice.

You see, meditation requires you to commit to the practice of it.

It requires you to make the time and the space to BE, to sit, to place your attention on the nothingness of your breath and to be present in the moment.

To be honest, it's too slow for me. I don't know if you've picked up on this fact about me so far, but I'm not the type to enjoy sitting still! I am more of a "moving meditation" kind of girl: give me dancing, exercising, driving or walking over a mindful meditation any day.

But here's the thing; I could get better at if I really, truly wanted to. If I committed to the practice and tried a little harder every day, I could improve.

This is where meditation and confidence align. At the end of the day, practicing meditation isn't about "arriving" somewhere – it isn't even about being "good" or "bad" at it. It's about practicing being aware, being here and now, being in the present moment.

Confidence is the same. You don't "get" confident.

Just as with mastering your own practice of meditation, mastering your own practice of confidence is something that takes time and that compounds. The more you inch towards making confident decisions, the more natural it becomes to keep making those decisions.

When my husband first started his journey with meditation, he had private sessions with a meditation teacher. He would learn about the breath, about his posture and about where to place his attention so he could "drop in" and really go deep within himself.

I remember him telling me how hard it was for him to "drop in" and to really let go of his attachment to his thoughts. He was studying so hard and seeking deep knowledge about the power of meditation.

He learned that sometimes, Zen masters and monks would be able to access a place of deep enlightenment – a place where they'd have a profound experience.

He wanted to go to that place. Baaaaad. It became his unquestionable goal. He tried and tried and practiced and practiced and over a period of months, he felt like he was getting closer.

One day in a session with his meditation teacher, he "got there."

He arrived! The place he had desired to access for so long, and he had finally done it – he reached the place of profound depth!

And the moment the thought popped into his head – *This is it!*

I am here! – he instantly dropped right out.

The feeling was gone and the "enlightenment" vanished into thin air.

He tried for months and months after that to "get there" again, but he never did. And after a while, he realized that the practice of meditation was never about "getting" anywhere, anyway. It wasn't about reaching a certain level of enlightenment or mastering a certain experience – it was about the commitment he had to practice all along.

He was never going to reach a place called "meditated."

Instead, he grows better at his practice of meditation every day.

Confidence is exactly the same. You are never going to reach a place called "confidence," but you can grow your ability to create confidence by practicing it every day.

That's why I call it a practice.

It's something you need to commit to – daily, hourly sometimes even moment to moment. There is no final destination; instead, there is a freedom and lightness that comes with living your life for you, and knowing that with every difficult moment or experience that you move through, you're growing stronger and deeper in your practice of confidence.

The more you commit to this practice, the better you get at it, but you never arrive.

There is always room for the up-leveling.

Practice
definition/noun

1. **The actual application or use** of an idea, belief, or method, as opposed to theories relating to it.

2. **The customary, habitual, or expected procedure** or way of doing of something.

3. **Repeated exercise** in or performance of an activity or skill so as to **acquire** or **maintain proficiency** in it.

WHY CONFIDENCE IS SO UNCOMFORTABLE

It's no secret that I would kind of love to become the next J-Lo, Oprah or female version of Tony Robbins (I actually have a slight obsession with all of these incredible people).

Most of us look at famous singers, movie stars and celebrities as if they have all the confidence in the world.

But by now, you're hopefully starting to appreciate that these people aren't confident because they're famous performers.

They have built incredible careers and lives for themselves because they are willing to feel the fear, the dread, the anxiety, the shame, the adversity and the impostor syndrome in the pits of their bellies… and they take the leap anyway.

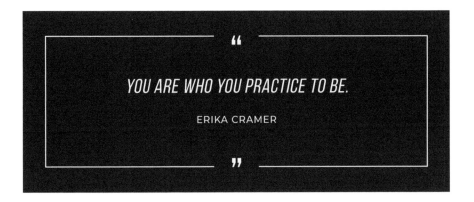

> **YOU ARE WHO YOU PRACTICE TO BE.**
>
> ERIKA CRAMER

Amazing things don't happen "to" them. They go out there, grab life by the horns and they make shit happen for themselves.

And they commit to the practice of confidence and taking risks every single day.

I mean, do you think it was easy for Oprah to become the woman she is today? She had to move through so much trauma from her past, she had to overcome the racist and sexist people who told her she wouldn't make it. She had to fight to be recognized and she had to continuously show up for herself along her entire career.

She never gave up on herself, and she used her resilience and her ability to overcome adversity. She struggled, she fell many times (often publicly) – yet there she is standing strong, changing the world with her vision, her mission and her purpose.

The reason why she and many others you look up to are "winning at life" is because they went for it. They pushed themselves to new and uncomfortable limits. They try new things, set the bar even higher, step outside their comfort zones on the daily, and they experiment (and "fail" – on the world stage, with all eyes on them!).

Do you think Jennifer Lopez is not shitting her pants the day she releases a new album?

And when her new music fails to set the charts on fire, do you think she's not devastated?

Of course she is!

But does she let an experience (or God forbid, a "failure") like that stop her from trying again? Nope. Not a chance. And that's what the practice of confidence is really all about.

Think about it: the very act of you being confident is you deciding to show up and do something out there, next level, scary, or nerve-racking and important. Most of the time your "call to confidence" comes when you're extremely nervous or unsure.

The entire time, you're likely to be feeling worried, scared, uncomfortable or dumb, or sitting in self-doubt about how it's going to go.

This is because you don't actually **feel** confident when you're **practicing** confidence.

You're actually moving through some of the most uncomfortable emotions when you're on your way to building confidence.

Keep in mind that confidence is an emotion, and as you've already learned in chapter three, emotions are generated based on the thoughts you're thinking.

When you're doing something scary, new or exciting, your thoughts are usually racing and future-focused. But you don't have to listen to them!

Instead when you are willing to experience these difficult and uncomfortable emotions – that's when you access the tools that lead to confidence.

It's not easy. But it will be worth it, as experiencing these emotions can and will only help you become stronger and more resilient.

I want to share an example about a goal I have personally that makes me shit myself with fear. Like, literally, I get nervous butterflies in my stomach just thinking about it…

I have always wanted to do a TED Talk. OMG, I get so nervous even just thinking about it. I'm sweating as I write this!

Why does it shake me? Well…first of all, I instantly think about and compare myself to the incomparable Dr. Brené Brown. Her amazing talk on vulnerability raised the bar HIGH.[10]

Second of all, you only have 18 minutes to talk. It can take me that long to get through an introduction.

Third, that damn red rug – something about it freaks me out.

As a result, I am petrified of ever even thinking about raising my hand to be considered to deliver a TED Talk.

Even though it's one of my biggest and deepest desires.

Sounds healthy, right?!

Here's where my work as a confidence coach comes in handy (because let me tell you, I do this work on myself ALL the time). So, let's unpack this a little.

First of all, there is my preconceived fear of doing a TED Talk. If I hold onto this fear, it's going to keep me from even applying. It will definitely stand in my way of attracting this opportunity so therefore, presenting on the TED stage would probably never happen.

Next, let's tackle that little old concern that I'm not going to live up to the standards set by Brené Brown…who just happens to be one of the most famous and well-respected speakers on the planet. (Girl, I know how to set high benchmarks, huh?!)

I mean, really?! She's Brené Brown and I am Erika Cramer: why would I compare myself to her groundbreaking TED Talk on vulnerability?!

It's like being a brand-new recording artist, about to release your very first single, and worrying that it won't be as good as Beyoncé. It is not helpful AND it won't allow me to stand in my message and deliver what the audience needs to hear – plus, comparing myself to her will only keep me more in fear, and in why I shouldn't apply (what I like to call the "I'm not good enough" spiral).

Next, let's chat about that red rug. Since I've watched so many TED Talks and I know how amazing it would be to give one and how important it is to me to do a "good job," that red rug haunts me. I have let it become a symbol as to how I am just not good enough because I haven't conquered the red rug yet.

Do you hear the shitty beliefs, scary untrue stories and deep comparison happening here? Good!

So what's the reality? Well, I am going to apply – that's the reality!

I know deep inside that I can do it – that I can actually kill it, if I allow myself to give it a chance.

I know that I have something of value to say. I know that I could train myself to speak for 18 minutes, and I know that I could rewire how I see the red rug (as a symbol of empowerment and speaking my truth to those who need it, instead of a symbol of my "failure.")

Yet, even when I apply and they love my pitch and I get accepted… and on the day, I get ready, I choose my TED Talk outfit (no pressure!) and I drive to the venue and I walk into the building… even when all of that happens, and I get the opportunity to step up onto the TED Talk stage, and I take my place in the middle of the red rug and start speaking…

Even when ALL of that happens, on the day, I know I would absolutely shit myself.

I mean that literally. I would do a spiritual poo* FOR SURE, while I'm getting ready. And the second before stepping on the stage, my heart would be racing. My mouth would be dry. My palms would be clammy, my armpits would be sweaty and my hands would be shaking.

> "
> ## I KNOW DEEP INSIDE THAT I CAN DO IT – THAT I CAN ACTUALLY KILL IT, IF I ALLOW MYSELF TO GIVE IT A CHANCE.
> "

I would nervously smile as I walked out on the stage and I would look down at the red rug briefly, just for a second, and a flush of "holy fuck" would fill my body.

I would take a deep breath and I would begin speaking with a nervous, shaky voice that would (hopefully) settle after a minute or two.

---

* Spiritual poo is a term my gorgeous friend Tanja came up with. It's what happens when you find yourself feeling big time nervous, anxious, or about to dive into the unknown. It's usually a good sign that you're about to go to the next level of yourself.

Sounds like a fucking magical time, doesn't it?!

It would actually suck, in the sense that it would feel like shit…to begin with. But once I'm in flow and I'm in my groove, I know I'd kill it!

Then I'd dance off that stage and I'd jump up and down, smiling, laughing and reveling in how awesome it was.

I'd feel more confident because of what I did. And I would have leveled up just that little bit more, so I can raise the bar even higher for myself next time.

That's how the practice of confidence goes: before = scared, nervous, shaking, sweating, heart racing. After = feeling like a fucking boss with a hot pink cape on and a "C" for confidence across your chest.

We all have these moments. Moments where you feel super confident, where you feel incredible and on top of the world – and then a bird shits on your head.

Moments where you feel so good about yourself and the job you're doing at work – and then you get an email from your boss telling you how upset she is that you dropped the ball on the last project.

Moments where you feel like you found Mr./Mrs. Right because you had the most magical date and you both vibed so hard and had the best chemistry – then six days go by with no call or no text, and yup, you've been ghosted.

You can't hold on to the feeling of confidence, because it ebbs and flows and it's only created when you are in the practice of it, meaning, when you are showing up, making decisions, being brave, taking action, falling on your face or killing it…and either way, you commit to doing it all over again and again and again.

The women you look up to who you think are "confident"? They LIVE in this practice. This is their way of life. They do it so much and so well that you don't even realize they're in it; it may seem like they live in one massive confident moment, but that's not true. They get nervous and anxious and sweaty pits just as much as the next woman.

THE POWER OF MOMENTUM

When you get really good at practicing confidence, what you're really getting good at is momentum.

Momentum is an interesting thing – you can have momentum for positive things, like creating confidence and self-belief, or you can have momentum for negative things, like procrastination and self-sabotage. The less you do, the more down-spiraled momentum you get.

The reason why I call it a practice is because it takes commitment. It takes you getting back up every step of the way when you fall short – and isn't falling short the lesson? If you don't fall short, mess up and get it wrong, then you don't grow…and you wouldn't ever know what leveling up feels like.

We need all of these experiences to grow us. We need to fall flat on our asses and learn how to get back up again, so we can learn how to truly embody self-confidence.

We all know that we're going to fall or fail at some stage – that's a guarantee. But it's not about falling; it's about getting back up, quickly, and without letting the fall stop you from moving forward.

I have a lot to say about failure as well but I'll save that for when we get into the 5 Cs.

YOU GET BETTER BY REPETITION.

You gain confidence by practicing

CONSISTENTLY.

— ERIKA CRAMER —

HOW I BROKE THROUGH MY CONFIDENCE BARRIER

If you want to gain confidence, you know by now that you're playing the long game – there is no switch you can flick to gain this kind of inner self-love and acceptance overnight.

There is often a tipping point, though; a moment where we recognize, like, "Hey! I'm making some good progress here!"

For me, that moment came a few years ago when I first started my coaching business. I was committed to making my business work, but I won't sugarcoat it: we were in deep financial scarcity and struggle.

I had just given birth to our second son. My husband's gym was struggling and I had decided that I wasn't going back to my safe and financially secure corporate gig. We were in the worst financial position we had ever been in as a couple, and I knew that I needed to do everything I could to get my business "out there."

Success was the only option.

I found Gary Vaynerchuk and his life-changing book *Crushing It*[11] and from that point, EVERYTHING changed.

I started creating content like crazy. I did weekly Facebook lives, Instagram lives, I created YouTube videos, I started recording my podcast – you name it, I was all over it.

One day I received a Facebook message from a woman who had been following me for some time on social media.

She told me she loved my message and what I was all about, and that she worked for a local government council. She was running a massive women's event and she wanted me to come speak to a room full of small businesswomen on the topic of confidence.

I agreed and hung up the phone. "Holy shit babe – my first paid speaking offer!" I said to my husband.

"What the hell am I going to talk about?!"

I mean, yes, I was a confidence coach. And technically, I had launched a business that was all about helping women access their confidence.

But I had never before spoken to a room full of women to share my nuggets of wisdom on building confidence – In fact, I had never been booked officially as a confidence professional (ahem) for a paid gig before!

I instantly went into imposter syndrome mode. That's a polite way of saying: I freaked the fuck out.

OMG, I don't know what I am doing. What am I going to talk about? What if I bomb it? What if none of the women get anything out of it? Why did I say yes to this when I clearly don't know enough…?!

My husband, being the amazing creature that he is, calmed me down and reassured me that if they had contacted me, they wanted my vibe and they wanted me to be "me" in all my flavor.

This gave me a little bit of comfort.

That night when the kids were in bed, we sat down at the dinner table and created a master plan.

And he asked me one of the most important questions I had ever been asked about confidence:

"If you were to explain how to be more confident to your best friend, what would you say?"

It got me thinking. I got our big whiteboard out and I wrote and scribbled, erased and wrote again, thinking about the things that confident people do and how they show up.

Bit by bit, it came together as a step-by-step process. After two hours of brainstorming and whiteboard scribbles, I had it: five core things. These are the five steps that all confident people follow. They're the five steps that I personally moved through to become the Erika that I am today – the five core things that I still do and practice now on the daily, as the "Queen of Confidence" founder.

"This is the process," I nodded to Hamish as the clock ticked past midnight. "And it's also my new keynote presentation for my first ever paid speaking gig! What should I call it?"

"Simple," he replied. "It's the Art of Practicing Confidence."

It was perfect.

Now I had my keynote presentation ready to go. What I hadn't quite yet mastered was the confidence in myself to deliver it.

" IF YOU WERE TO EXPLAIN HOW TO BE MORE CONFIDENT TO YOUR BEST FRIEND, WHAT WOULD YOU SAY? "

Have you ever regretted so badly saying yes to something that you'd give anything, ANYTHING at all, to get out of the situation you find yourself in?

Yup, that was how I felt right before that speaking event.

The day finally came where I had to give my keynote on "the art of practicing confidence."

There I found myself, in the bathroom of a fancy hotel, stressing the hell out, feeling sick to my stomach and literally wanting to time travel to the next day, so I could put this moment behind me and this whole thing would just be OVER!

That morning, there were 75 women gathered in the ballroom of a 5-star hotel, waiting for me to tell them how to become more confident.

And there I was, doing a spiritual poo in the toilet stall and praying to the Gods to get me outta this place.

To paint the picture of how haywire my day had been, let me set the scene. This was my vision for how things would go when I'd said yes to the event weeks earlier:

I'd give my son a feed (I was still breastfeeding) and then he'd be happy to let my mother-in-law look after him for a few hours while I got ready, prepared and presented to the crowd.

I'd have plenty of time to calmly put my face on so I looked fresh and flawless. I'd curl my hair and dress in something that made me feel confident, skinny and amazing (even though I didn't feel confident in my post-baby body at the time).

I'd get there early enough to mingle and chat with twenty-five percent of the room, so I could feel them out and make some friends I could later connect eyes with when I was on stage (in case a joke bombed and I needed some semi-familiar smiling faces).

Then I'd step on stage, wow the crowd with my insights, ideas and funny jokes, and leave the event feeling like a total bad-ass who has my shit together and wasn't an imposter AT ALL.

In reality? The morning was an absolute shit-show. AND it was raining! (Damn, I had curled my hair for this?!)

The truth is, as soon as I said yes to speaking at this event, I thought: "FUCK! I should have said no. I can't do this."

I'd just had a baby and I was so damn tired. My boobs were massive and I only had about 1.5 hours after feeding my son before they felt like milk bombs about to explode in my dress (true story).

My reality at that moment was that I felt ANYTHING but confident.

And since it was the first real speaking job I had ever been booked for, I was running this story in my head that I wasn't "professional enough" and that I wasn't enough of an expert to do this keynote.

I literally had to Google "what's the difference between a talk and a keynote" three days before the event!

There were going to be 75 businesswomen in that room, but it might as well have been millions of people to me – in that moment I didn't think I could provide them with any value as a presenter, and I was shitting myself about it (literally).

I had never done this before, therefore, as I was preparing for the event, I had a full on "Who the fuck do I even think I am?" imposter syndrome moment.

I couldn't believe that it was the morning of this important event and nothing went to plan.

It was raining, I was running late, my baby didn't want to feed (so there goes my kid-free time to calmly get ready). I couldn't zip up my dress, my boobs were so engorged, I hated my frizzy hair and I was stressed the fuck out.

Not the best way to kick off a speaking gig about confidence, huh?

I was so disorganized and chaotic that instead of arriving 30 minutes early and giving myself time to prepare and connect with the ladies, I was rushed and flustered and arrived at the hotel just a few minutes before I was due on stage.

In actual fact, they had wanted me to start a little early – which I would have known, if I'd gotten there half an hour early as planned and I hadn't been running so damn late!

I was literally running into the hotel.

My husband dropped me off in the parking lot and I ran to the elevator (mind you, I had my jeans and t-shirt on since my plan was to get dressed at the venue in a calm, unhurried way).

There I am, hopping into the elevator, literally putting my earrings on and rushing to the stage. A few ladies in the elevator even asked me if I was going to the businesswomens' event?

I had to say, "Um, yes…I am actually the speaker…"

I felt like a fraud. It was the worst. I tried to keep it together, but I was so overwhelmed. I was anxious and rushed (and looked nothing like my pretty, polished image in the flyer.)

The story I kept telling myself that morning?

It went something like this: *Who the fuck am I to talk to women about having their shit together?! Or having confidence? I don't even have my shit together right now. Erika, sista – you don't have this. You're gonna fuck up big time.*

Confidence
is a
practice;
one you must
commit to
daily, hourly,
sometimes
even
**moment to
moment.**

ERIKA CRAMER

I SHOULD HAVE SAID "NO"

I should have turned down the opportunity.

That's how I felt in the moment.

It would have been so much *easier* NOT to do it.

I could have stayed at home in my sweatpants and relaxed with no pressure. I could have fed my baby when he was ready, taken all the stress off myself and played it safe.

I swear to God, in the minutes before I went on stage, I had to really dig deep and I had to take my own advice. The five-step process that I had created for this specific event was starting to come in really handy because I was feeling anything but confident!

This shitshow of a morning definitely required me to step into my own practice. I knew I had to stop believing the bullshit story that I was feeding myself – the one that said I wasn't good enough, that I couldn't deliver and that I didn't deserve to be there.

So I locked myself in the toilet down the hall and I took some deep breaths. I looked in the mirror and I said to myself: "You can do this. They asked you to do this because you can."

I did a spiritual poo and quite literally flushed the nerves out of my system. (And I instantly felt better – what is it about a nervous poo that feels so freeing?!)

I quickly touched up my makeup (red lips to get me out of my funk), shoved my engorged boobs back into my bra, squeezed myself into some spanx, put my dress on and climbed into some very high cheetah print heels (not gonna lie, those heels made me feel pretty damn great about myself).

I walked into the room all smiles. Everyone was already seated, (ugh!) so I tried to make eye contact with as many ladies as I could on my way to my table.

Then when the MC introduced me, I did what I know to do best... I kept it real.

I jumped up on that stage and immediately told all the women that my boobs were exploding with milk as my baby had refused to feed, and that I only had 60 minutes before the ladies in the front row may or may not get sprayed. I told them that I got caught in the rain and my hair and face melted, and I admitted that I had "met a few of you in the elevator as I was half-dressed, putting my earrings on."

Then, I told them that I had just done a spiritual poo because I was so nervous.

Yup. I said that.

And do you know what they did? They cracked up laughing!

They were in tears. Literally, howling with laughter.

It was great – it was actually the greatest thing ever.

It just so happened that my real AF situation made them all laugh, because most of them actually understood what I had been through. Plus, they were shocked at how real and brutally honest I was. The pretty, perfectly polished "Confidence Coach" rocking up and admitting she's an imperfect hot mess!

No one quite expected that. But, it was the truth.

I couldn't sit up there and pretend that my morning didn't just go to shit – I had to keep it real with them.

By making myself vulnerable, I broke the ice and helped them feel seen. I also re-set my expectations of myself – because I realized that I didn't have to be perfect up on that stage.

They weren't expecting perfection.

And I mean, hello! I was literally teaching them what practicing confidence actually looked like by being the LIVE example. That vulnerable and raw opening ended up being a great (and real) segue into my keynote on what confidence really looks and feels like.

Needless to say, the event went really well and afterwards, so many women came up to me and told me how much they'd enjoyed it. Many of the women commented that it was a breath of fresh air to see another woman be so real, so relatable, vulnerable and hilarious. I was on top of the world and I was so proud of myself for pushing ahead.

I'm not even kidding: 10 minutes before the event, I was so stressed out and worried that it would be a total flop.

But 10 minutes afterwards, I felt alive, vibrant and energized. I couldn't wait to book another event. I couldn't wait to do this again. As it turns out, that event was the catalyst for my speaking style: a mixture of edutainment, inspiring stories and a confidence comedy show!

What happened next? Well, I drove home (buzzing), breastfed my baby (finally!), stripped out of my gorgeous but uncomfortable dress and kicked off my sexy but uncomfortable stilettos, and went back to being a mom in a breast milk-stained t-shirt looking after her kids. You know, the glam life.

And this, my love, is practicing confidence.

It's fleeting and it's hard work and it's book-ended by opportunities to level up, and those moments will push you so far out of your comfort zone that you'll want to turn away. But if you show up and push through, the wins make it so worth it.

They help you achieve more, experience more, accomplish what you desire and simply live more than you ever imagined possible.

In these moments you build resilience, grit, strength, momentum, consistency and then, ta-da!

Here comes your confidence.

Please don't expect for a second that it should be easy. Remember every single emotion I faced prior to the event? I was in so much discomfort it wasn't even funny. I felt horrible, sick to my stomach, anxious, frustrated, flustered and I was freaking the fuck out.

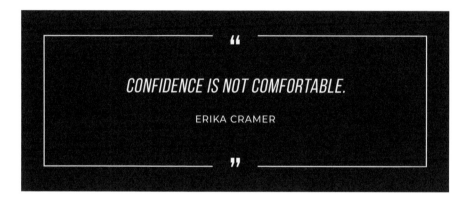

> ## CONFIDENCE IS NOT COMFORTABLE.
>
> ERIKA CRAMER

Nothing about this was nice and easy.

If (scratch that – when!) I reach my goal of delivering a TED Talk or being interviewed by Oprah (hey, you've gotta dream BIG!), I'm sure I will be just as nervous and the lead up to the event will be every bit as horrendous as that day was.

But afterwards, I'm sure I'll feel ten times as elated, proud and energized as I was that day.

Because it is only AFTER we show up and go for it (whatever "it" is) that we feel confident and able to celebrate ourselves.

Now, back to those five core tenets of confidence that I mentioned earlier. These are the five steps that all confident people follow – and in the coming chapters, you're going to learn all about them.

EP #44

They represent the foundations of the practice of confidence, which I call the 5 Cs, and you'll soon be able to see that these are the steps that all "confident" women take. Most importantly, you'll be able to use this process to create confidence for yourself on the daily.

The great thing about the practice is that when you get stuck (and you will get stuck), all you have to do is keep going. The next step is your way through.

Let me be super clear here…the 5 Cs are not some revolutionary shit either. It's a five-step process that absolutely has the power to help you uplevel in every area and go for what you want in your life, but it's based on really simple principles.

Sometimes, it's the simplest things that can have the biggest impact.

But just because something is simple – that doesn't mean it's easy.

As you move through the 5 Cs, you will begin to create your confidence. Whilst there's never a moment where you arrive at "confidence," because it's a constant process of creating your own momentum, you will notice that the more you do it, the more you take action, the more you shit yourself but show up anyway… then the more you'll learn from your mistakes, the more you'll continue to show up, the more you will practice and the more confidence you will create.

After consistent practice – the 5 Cs can become your default mode.

This is the secret to confidence and the secret to you creating your confidence. It all starts here… 👑

CHAPTER 6

THE 5 Cs

—

choice

CONFIDENCE *isn't* CREATED IN ~~comfort~~ ZONES

— ERIKA CRAMER —

It all starts here. To walk through life with confidence, first and foremost you need to acknowledge that you have choices. You have free will to *choose* what you want or don't want and whether you realize it or not, you are making dozens of choices on the daily.

The question is: are the choices you're making leading you towards empowering decisions? Or have your choices been keeping you in fear?

This is the first part of creating confidence and it's step one of the practice, because truly effective decision-making can only come from a place of empowering CHOICES.

Every single one of us, every single day in every single moment, has the ability to make a decision. This is one of our many choices. Choice and decision go hand-in-hand when it comes to you practicing confidence.

When we aren't actively choosing to make decisions for the things that matter most to us, we end up idle…this is when we "wish" things would change and "hope" for more in our lives, but we haven't actually DECIDED to choose something better for ourselves.

A classic example of this is wanting to lose weight. How many of us have committed to changing the way we eat? "The diet starts on Monday," we promise, and in that moment, we are making the choice to lose weight. But when it comes to deciding what to eat for dinner on Friday night, we reach for that third slice of pizza or order another glass of wine.

In other words – the *decision* that we make doesn't line up with our *choice*.

This is also where "procrastination station," "analysis paralysis" and self-sabotage tend to kick in. And where we can unconsciously fall into the trap of comparison and judgment of ourselves and of others – thinking that it may be others are "just born with self-confidence."

In reality it's not easier for anyone else than it is for you; they are just deciding to move through the practice. They are making choices and deciding to act on their life, instead of watching it pass by and giving reasons why it's not working out the way they wanted.

Here's what I know: if you picked up this book and you have even the slightest interest in gaining more self-confidence, then I can bet there is a decision that you have been putting off. A decision that you haven't yet committed to making.

Maybe you've thought about making the decision in your head, but that's not gonna cut it, is it? A decision made in your head is not a decision made. It's a thought that you've thought about. A "maybe it would sound nice to do that?"

But you haven't actually chosen to make that decision and you haven't truly decided that you want to go for this, whatever it is.

When you choose to make a decision, you DO something – you act on it.

It's instant.

It's automatic.

It's happening right now.

You don't have to wait 10 years to decide; you don't have to wait until something finally changes, your children grow up, you move to a different location, you have more money, you have better family support, the list goes on…These are all most likely just reasons why you're not choosing, but reasons don't get you the results you want.

As the amazing Tony Robbins says: "Our culture teaches us that making significant changes takes a long time and is difficult to do.

EP #167

This is simply NOT true. Change happens in an instant. It is not a process – it is something you do in an instant, by simply making a decision."[12]

The reality is that you can choose to decide right now. The only thing stopping you is your story about why you can't.

The first choice you need to make is to decide! It sounds funny, right?

But honestly, that's all there is to it – instead of procrastinating on this little choice, just decide that you're going to start moving in the direction of what you desire.

Decide that you are going to finally go for and create what you want.

It has to start there.

Many times, we don't choose what we actually, really want for fear of thinking we won't really get it. We don't dream or go for scary goals because deep down, we don't believe we can achieve these things, it may seem impossible at times. So instead we don't show up, we hide and we let our fear guide us back to the similar results we've always gotten.

> ❝
>
> # THE REALITY IS THAT YOU CAN CHOOSE TO DECIDE RIGHT NOW. THE ONLY THING STOPPING YOU IS YOUR STORY ABOUT WHY YOU CAN'T.
>
> ❞

When you stop making decisions, you stop taking action towards the things you want to create.

If you don't make these decisions, you have to accept that the things you want to happen in your life can't happen.

If you want to become more confident, if you want to feel empowered and on purpose you must choose to start doing so.

When you make these choices to put your desires first, you are able to move in the direction of what you want.

You're able to start kicking goals and doing the things that are important to YOU.

Decision-making is about being clear about your values, knowing what's important to you and prioritizing that.

So many of us lack clarity on what really matters to us and when we're in this space, we allow ourselves to get pushed and pulled according to other people's wants and desires.

Think about it: how many times have you agreed to plans that you weren't that excited about, said yes to help someone with something you didn't really want to do, or let someone else choose something on your behalf because you lacked any real conviction to say what is it YOU wanted?

So consider: what do you value? What's important to you?

Are you prioritizing your desires and your happiness, or are you following in the footsteps of what other people have told you that you "should" do?

When you put things off or put your own needs last, you only delay your happiness.

Plus, you are always making a decision – you may not be making a choice to do what you want, but trust me, decisions are happening!

You are deciding to live in mediocrity; you're deciding to settle for less; you're deciding to procrastinate and self-sabotage for fear of what may happen if you do the scary things you keep avoiding.

Choice is about you being honest with what you want and being committed to do what it takes to get it.

Choice is about you realizing that you have a choice and that your desires matter, that YOU matter!

Choice allows you to take your power and responsibility back – after all, you get to call the shots in YOUR life.

THIS IS WHAT IT LOOKS LIKE WHEN YOU *DON'T* STEP INTO <u>CHOICE</u>

When you decide not to make active choices, there are consequences.

Here are some of the things you could find yourself doing…

SELF-SABOTAGING ♕

You know what you want, but you keep repeating the same shitty patterns and making poor choices derived from fear, which then keeps you in fear and a lack of responsibility. This results in you not creating the confidence to go for what you want. Maybe you're ready to take on some more responsibility at work and step into that leadership role, but instead of putting your hand up in the meeting, you sit there quietly. And instead of speaking up when your boss asks for someone to take the lead on something, you shy away once again, letting your fear hold you back from going for what you truly want. So you stay in that position that you know you dislike, when you know you're capable of more, and you're not happy – you're staying because it's easier to do what you know, than it is to step into the (at times scary) unknown.

PROCRASTINATING 👑

Putting things off is normal and natural, but it becomes a problem when it gets to a point where the overwhelm and lack of action itself keeps you in a lack of action. It's a vicious cycle of anxiety and inaction. If you're procrastinating, you may be extremely overwhelmed with "all of the things" you need to do, yet you don't CHOOSE one or commit to following through on anything. Maybe you've had a minor task that you keep putting off: let's say organizing your kid's birthday party. It's weeks away, so you don't worry about it yet…then as the date approaches, you get overwhelmed and anxious just thinking about all the little things that need to get done. The cake, the decorations, the food (all the allergies of the kids who are coming) then you have the venue, the toys, the activities…Before you know it, you've spiraled into anxiety and nothing's gotten done – or worse, you focus on the tiny, easy stuff that doesn't really make a difference to the overall project. If this goes unchecked you can self-loathe, sit in guilt and sometimes even depression.

BEING CHRONICALLY INDECISIVE 👑

Where you're so unsure of yourself that you always ask others for their opinion or advice. Or, you have many ideas but you do nothing about them, as you get too overwhelmed with all of the options and shiny objects that may come your way. When you wait for others to decide for you, you don't get to gain the resilience that comes from making the wrong choice. You will one hundred percent make choices that are "wrong," by the way! You have to, in order to learn what is right for you. This is the beauty of duality – you don't know what is "right" if you never experience what is "wrong." When you try to protect yourself from making any wrong decisions or any outcome that's not perfect, you rob yourself of the experience itself. Not only that, but you can become needy and someone who is constantly seeking validation and approval of others – if this goes unchecked it can hurt your self-worth big time. This also leads back to you sabotaging yourself and or procrastinating, as these are all connected.

WHEN YOU STOP
MAKING DECISIONS,

*you stop
taking action*

TOWARDS THE
THINGS YOU WANT
TO CREATE.

— ERIKA CRAMER —

LIVING IN FEAR 👑

Here is where every one of these ties together. There are really only two emotions: love or fear. At the end of the day when you're not doing what you want to do (or living the life you know you deserve to live), you're operating from FEAR. When you're operating in fear you often end up attracting the exact thing you're in fear of, because you're so focused on it. Fear of failure is the most common one. You may feel worried that if you go for the things you truly desire to have and fail, you won't recover. When you have a fear of failure you rarely "just go for it" because the fear of you failing doesn't even allow for you to try. The fear of success is another big one: if you try to work towards something you want and you actually succeed, how is that going to change how you see yourself, how you identify yourself? It sounds silly but it's true, as so many of us worry about how it will affect our relationships, our friendships, our lifestyle, how other people perceive us? I personally believe that this one is the one we struggle with the most. What if we were, as Marrianne Williamson so beautifully said: "powerful beyond measure"? Can you imagine a world where women believed they were "powerful beyond measure," a world where YOU believed you were POWERFUL BEYOND MEASURE?

I hope you're starting to see how even when you think you're not actively choosing, decisions are being made.

And these decisions are most likely not giving you the outcomes and results you want. Hence why you need to start choosing!

You can either consciously choose to go for the goals and dreams you desire to create OR you can keep letting your subconscious, default, autopilot fear-mode choose.

IF NOT NOW, THEN WHEN?

When I became a stylist, I didn't fully commit to it in the beginning. Instead, it was my side-hustle (for five years mind you). I worked full-time for a hair and beauty retail company, and on the weekends, I would run styling events for groups of women.

It lit me up to be surrounded by women and to be doing work that helped them feel good about themselves. But a part of me didn't really care about the fashion side of things, or teaching them about the external, material, surface elements of confidence.

I was so interested in speaking to them about internal confidence.

I wanted to help my clients think better thoughts and question their negative beliefs so they could feel better about themselves. At that point, I was in the thick of my own journey, of healing my past and working with mentors and coaches. I was learning so much about myself, especially when it had to do with my mindset and the way I saw myself.

Every time I ran a styling event, I would end up weaving some kind of coaching exercise into the mix and it would leave the women in tears. I mean they came to me for styling, and they often left crying and healing some parts of their past! I was finding that there was more to this thing called confidence. I discovered that there were layers, like an onion, when it came to helping women truly accept themselves and gain true confidence, and during this time I discovered the idea of internal and external confidence.

I was seeing how I would help my clients with their *external* layer of confidence. I would teach them how to buy nice clothes, wear flattering makeup, style their hair, how to dress in ways that would highlight their favorite bits and downplay their least favorite bits, and pull it all together with jewelry, bags and shoes. But, I soon realized that it wasn't enough. It was still the surface layer.

As I evolved personally through my own journey with coaches, mentors, seminars and programs; healing my own lack of self-belief and self-worth, I would bring this into my styling events.

I started focusing more on the *inner* confidence, teaching them about their limiting beliefs, their thoughts and how they have been treating themselves. I would include powerful (and very emotional) exercises throughout the styling event where they would have amazing personal breakthroughs.

The more I went into the inner confidence – culling the wardrobe of their thoughts, helping them change their inner dialogue and mindset – the more I realized how much I wanted to do this work with more women.

I stopped caring about the clothing and the hair accessories and I started seeing how much we women needed self-acceptance, sisterhood and self-belief.

I realized that I actually wanted to be a confidence coach and I wanted to share more about the journey towards inner confidence, but I had no idea where to start. And, I was still working my day job. AND with my one-on-one styling clients.

The more events that I ran, the more I dreamt of leaving my full-time job. Once I realized that I would never be truly happy at my day job, I made the choice to leave. I just knew I couldn't do it anymore. I also made the decision to stop styling and start coaching.

Believe me when I tell you – I was so scared. It was the most intense time to be making these big decisions. Financially, as I mentioned earlier, it was not the ideal time to quit my stable job and secure income.

We'd just had our second baby; Hamish's gym business wasn't doing very well at the time; we'd recently bought a new SUV and had moved into a new house we were renting. All of the expenses were mounting up as our bank account balance was declining into negative. Literally. At one point we were searching for coins under the seat of our car to buy bread.

This was our lowest financial point as a couple and since we'd had our second child, we honestly felt like we were going backwards. I mean, I had struggled in poverty in America growing up and this was **nothing** like that – but this was our lowest low as grown-ups and definitely the lowest I had experienced while living in Australia.

It was worse because we "knew" better than to be in this position, yet there we were. The financial stress was real and the pressure was *on*.

I was in the shower one night (why does all the wisdom come in the shower?) and I heard the voice clearly. "What does the Queen of Confidence do? She talks about confidence. She doesn't talk about cotton, linen or horizontal stripes – she talks about confidence."

I ran downstairs half-naked and still dripping wet from the shower. It was like a lightbulb moment for me and I couldn't wait any longer.

I told my husband then and there that I couldn't do styling anymore and I was quitting my full-time job. He was shocked, to say the least; not only did I want to quit my day job, but I also wanted to let go of my paid side-hustle when we were in deep financial struggle.

I was panting and my hands were shaking, because every single part of me knew this was the right answer – it just felt like the wrong time. I knew it was risky, but I also knew I literally had to make this choice. Although this really wasn't the best time to leave my secure and safe (well-paying) job to go create a brand new coaching business, I was sick of putting my dreams and desires on hold and I knew that I just couldn't do another styling event – I was done.

Could I have waited until my kids were older, or we were in a better financial position, or until we reworked our finances, or until the gym was getting busier?

Yup. Absolutely. I could have easily put it off for a later, more convenient time.

But I knew it was important and I knew I had to make that choice then and there, or else I maybe never would. And my life would be okay, it would be fine…but I wouldn't be putting myself or my desires first. If I continued down that path, I probably would have ended up resenting my husband eventually as well…

The cost of me not making this decision was HUGE. For so long, I wished that things were different. I compared myself to others, I felt like others were "lucky" and I wasn't.

And it was costing me my life's purpose, my financial freedom and my children seeing their mother do work that lights her up and sets her soul on fire.

I had found my big decision and it was a scary and very risky one – but I knew that the only way I was going to feel aligned, happy and on purpose was if I went for it.

The only way to do that was to dive head-first into making my dreams a reality.

Now, I am not telling you to quit your job and hope for the best – no way! What I did was communicate deeply with my husband, then I transitioned all of my styling clients over to my confidence coaching business; thankfully each of them told me they needed more confidence if they were ever going to feel good in their clothing (I guess my Styling Confidently events had worked!) so I had a big pool of clients to keep me going. I also got on the phone with my mentor and worked out a game plan on how I would leave my full-time job, but still create a side income casually. All of this meant we had some money coming in while I started HUSTLING and building my coaching business from scratch – after all, we did have two kids and bills to pay, so we needed a plan if I was going to go all in. What I'm saying is that I had every excuse in the world to "wait," but instead of using those as excuses, I found a way to do it NOW.

OVER TO YOU...

What is your current reality?

Where do you need to make a decision in your life that is impacting your happiness?

Where do you need to **step up** so that you can **step into** your confidence?

What have you been putting off for **fear of failure**, or **fear of being seen**, or being **perfect**?

Do you hate your job? Are you sick of staying in relationships that don't make you happy? Are you over getting disrespected by your in-laws?

Maybe you need to finally let go of that frenemy who criticizes you on the daily?

IS THERE A CHOICE YOU NEED TO MAKE?

IS THERE A DECISION THAT NEEDS YOUR ATTENTION?

If you're currently here, in step one – Choice, here's my **loving bitch slap** to get you moving to the next step:

Get a piece of paper, or better yet a book (and no, a Kmart receipt won't cut it here sister)! I want you to start writing your answers to these questions down below.

It's time to get it out on paper!

You may find exactly what your next move is, if you allow yourself the freedom to write what you actually want. Let it flow, filter and judgment-free. It doesn't even have to make sense.

Don't let your mind tell you that bullshit "I don't know" story – the one that has kept you playing small for far too long now. What do you really want? What do you desire? What kind of life do you want to have? What have you dreamed about? What sparks envy in you when you see someone else has it?

(This is a gift, by the way – seeing someone else achieve a goal and feeling that flare of jealousy means you've just identified a future goal or desire for yourself!)

So, what is it? What's that scary thing that when you think about actually going for this, it makes you have skid marks in your undies? That you're like, oh my God, I don't know if I could have it? I don't know if I could do it?

Don't worry about the "what if…" or the HOW – just let yourself dream big here for a moment.

Get out of your head and get into your body, get into your imagination…

Write it out now. All the ideas. All the dreams and desires.

Now is your time to do it. No more messing around. Let's go:

What do you really want for yourself, for your life?

What have you been putting off and neglecting?

Why are you not making the choice to put your happiness first?

What are you really scared of?

You'll start to see some common threads appear. And then, you keep writing it out – and consider, what is it that you are allowing to hold you back from choosing what you want?

What is it costing you to sit there in uncertainty and indecision? What is it costing your loved ones?

How could your life be different if you actually chose to go for what you wanted?

What if you backed yourself and made the decision you have been avoiding for so long? What if it changes your life forever?

What if all the happiness you desire were just one choice away? 👑

BREAK IN CASE OF EMERGENCY!

⚡ Feeling stuck? Flip back to pages 119-120 and try doing the exercize in Chapter Four about fear and intuition. It will help you realize that you can't make the wrong choice – because even the "wrong" one leads you to the right path.

⚡ Let go of the need to make the "perfect" choice (that doesn't exist) and instead, you need to trust the process and trust yourself here.

⚡ Also notice where you're asking others to choose for you, or where you're waiting for something to happen or change. There is never a "perfect" time to do anything, and if you are avoiding your choices and/or making excuses as to why you can decide right now, then you are standing in your own way.

⚡ Don't let overthinking stop you from moving forward. Keep in mind that if you get stuck here, it could be because you haven't decided to actually DO something...

⚡ Lastly, remember you are always choosing. The lack of a choice is a choice towards something. The question is: are the choices you're making right now leading you to the results you actually want?

MAY YOUR CHOICES REFLECT YOUR HOPES, NOT YOUR FEARS.

— NELSON MANDELA —

SAMANTHA GASH

CONFIDENCE FEELS LIKE SH*T

"I've spent over a decade connecting my passion of endurance and adventure as a vehicle for social change. It's through exploration and the broadening of my experience base, that I've discovered what confidence really is. Particularly in spaces that are unfamiliar to me, where I've felt challenged and even fear, I've discovered that the more I do, the more my self-belief grows. I also know my capacity to survive even when things don't go to plan.

We often forget how resilient human beings are. We don't need to go on a quest to find our resilience for the first time, it's already there inside us. We may just need to access it again.

The micro decisions we make every day can make a huge impact on our goals and dreams. When I am preparing any long term goal – from an expedition across a country to devising a social impact campaign, I break it into small manageable pieces. Then I decide how much time I am willing to spend on each little piece and what skills I or another team member can bring to it. Based on those decisions of time and skills, I then craft realistic stretch goals. I am a big proponent of setting myself up for growth but also success.

Don't forget that every goal you craft can have an impact on other people. That can be a really positive thing, as it immediately places people to be in your support team and gives you extra accountability. We are often more inclined to let ourselves down than other people. Don't be afraid to ask for help, lean on your people in the challenging times and celebrate the small wins along the way."

SAMANTHA GASH
Endurance athlete, speaker and social entrepreneur

Courage is resistance to fear, mastery of fear –

not absence of fear.

MARK TWAIN

CHAPTER 7

THE 5 Cs

—

courage

Courage is one of the most important parts of creating confidence. It is *THE* thing that gets us through uncertainty and it also goes hand-in-hand with choice – it almost feels like they happen at the same time!

The thing about courage is that it doesn't come to you unless you actually do the scary thing...in other words, you don't muster up the courage to do the courageous thing. It doesn't work like that. Instead, the courage comes AFTER you have made the choice to just fucking go for it, regardless of the fear and the unknowing.

Just as confidence will not come until you start practicing it (you don't get *confidence to be confident*), your courage won't come without you being courageous.

So what does it mean to be courageous? This is what courage is: it's when you do something, even though you are literally shitting yourself about it. I mean it, like the new definition of courage should be:

Courage

definition/noun

The feeling of pee dripping down your leg and or skid marks in your undergarments while you are doing something you are super shit scared to do.

CONFIDENCE FEELS LIKE SH*T

This is courage! It is pee dripping down your leg in nerves, maybe all the way down to your ankle, and it's butterflies having a dance party in your stomach, and it's trips to the toilet to unleash a spiritual poo.

You are nervous. You are scared. You are freaking out. But you move forward anyway.

You remember my story about wanting to do the TED Talk? How clammy my hands will be, how nervous I'll be stepping onto that stage? That's it! I mean, intellectually, I know that courage will not just "instantly" come to me the moment I walk on stage. But I also know that I need to act, to apply, to go for it, to stand on that little red rug…even though I am scared. Especially because I am scared!

Courage is all about you taking action, despite the fear.

It is about moving forward and making progress while you are simultaneously shitting yourself. So much fun, right?!

Sometimes, it can feel like courage is jumping off the cliff of indecision with no wings, with no parachute and no "Plan B."

You walk to the edge of the cliff on shaky legs, looking down, wondering what the hell will happen if you jump. If you stay perched on the edge for too long, you'll either shit yourself or talk yourself out of it.

So, you jump…

Holy shit! Holy shit! Holy shit!

You're screaming as you fall, wondering if you're crazy for jumping, hoping that you grow wings before you hit the bottom.

Can a human even grow wings? Is this possible? Am I nuts?!

"I have no parachute, I have no wings, I have no safety net…BUT, I believe my wings can come. I believe that I will not fall. I believe that I can do this."

And then all of a sudden, because you have the epic self-belief and because you've burned all the boats, you've backed yourself and you've jumped…you fucking grow wings right before you hit the bottom.

That's what courage is.

You don't come crashing down – you fucking grow wings!

This is obviously metaphorical; do not go jumping off any cliffs ladies, as far as I'm aware, doctors haven't discovered any secret wing chambers in our spines. But it's a powerful reminder that creating courage means truly backing yourself, one hundred percent.

For instance, this was how I felt when I quit my job at the worst possible time for my family from a financial perspective. It was a big risk to leave secure employment so I could launch my business as a Confidence Coach. As I mentioned, I was responsible about it – I transferred some styling clients to my new biz and I had some side-income coming in.

But I didn't try to start my business while still working full-time – I quit right away.

> ## COURAGE IS ALL ABOUT YOU TAKING ACTION, DESPITE THE FEAR.

And I didn't wait twelve months so I could build up some savings – I had no financial safety net.

And that gave me the determination, the motivation and the drive to make this work at all costs. I poured my heart and soul into this business because I knew that I could change lives, if I could just make this business work and find my tribe…

When you're doing something new, you're supposed to be nervous, you're supposed to be scared, you're supposed to be wondering if you're going to be okay, or if this is the "right" thing to do.

If you're someone who identifies as a "control freak," it's even scarier for you! Because courage is about stepping into the unknown; it's like walking in the dark and not knowing what the end result will be.

You can't ever know for sure what will happen, but if you don't stand in courage and if you don't give it a chance, you risk not knowing what could have been either.

THE MAGIC OF SURRENDER

Most of the time when we're doing something that makes us really scared or nervous, our natural instinct is to reject the unknown – that magical place where great things happen, but where we don't always control how things unfold.

I want to share a visual exercise with you to help you imagine what courage looks like. Imagine you're walking across a field through a thick fog. It's hard to see anything below your ankles and you can barely see two steps ahead of you. You *really* want to get to the other side of the field, but to do so, you have to surrender to the unknown – you literally have no idea what lies in front of you.

Poisonous snakes? Maybe. Fallen logs and tree branches? Possibly. A clear, flat path free of any tripping hazards? Could be!

You're freaked out, because you literally can't see shit. I can already hear the control freaks saying, "No, no, no, Erika! You've got to be kidding. How will I walk if I can't see my next steps? What if I trip on something? What if I get hurt?"

I get it. It's scary. But it can also be magical, exhilarating and life-changing. This is the unknown – and courage is all about embracing and surrendering fully to that which we don't always know.

Here's the thing: you can't know what lies ten steps ahead. Or even two steps ahead. You actually don't get the privilege of knowing any of that until you start walking.

When you commit to walking with courage, you don't know exactly what's going to happen. All you know is that you made the choice, the decision in step one – and now you've gotta muster up the courage to go forward into the thick fog WITHOUT seeing the whole picture.

You commit to moving forward and just taking the next step, without having an overview of exactly how every single step will look, or an inventory of every single thing you may (or may not) come across while you're walking.

Sometimes, you won't even know if you're actually on the right path.

So you have two choices.

You can play it safe and stall; stay put, exactly where you are, worrying about how much fog there is and how many risks lie ahead. You can then choose not to make a move, because you'd rather live with the "known" parameters of the tiny two-feet-squared space you currently occupy, even if you're not all that happy there.

Or…

You can accept the fact that you can't see very well. That you *might* trip on a rock or fall into a ditch. But at least you'll be moving:

slowly, carefully, with awareness of upcoming hazards, but without letting fear of potential problems stop you in your tracks.

You can pre-plan and work it out in advance as much as you can, but with courage, there comes a time when you actually need to surrender.

There is no secure and safe GPS map that guarantees you won't trip over in the fog. You just have to move. You have to walk. You need to do this scary, unknown thing.

How?

You put one foot in front of the other. Once you take the first step you start to notice that a few more steps become visible. How much? A little bit, that's all. That's all you can see at first, just a few steps in front of you. But the more you walk, the more the fog opens up and shows you more of the trail ahead.

Then, all of a sudden, you come across a path. And now you have more options: you can go left or right, or straight ahead. These paths are much clearer as the fog seems to be lifting, but you do have more choices to make.

You get more options and more clarity as you walk and as you take more steps, more courage gets built. Your path becomes clearer and clearer, your route starts to become more familiar, and now you can see so much more – the fog becomes a mist.

As you start gaining more confidence in yourself, sooner or later, you're not worried about falling over or tripping, as you've gained some great momentum and now the fog has cleared. You also know that if you trip and fall, you can pick yourself back up again…

The bottom line? You don't get the courage you want by *wishing* you were more courageous. You will not be courageous until you walk through that scary unknown fog and earn it.

This is what courage is about. And that's why so many people don't do it, because they don't like the unknown.

You see, we want to know what happens when we decide to go on that specific path. We want to know if we're going to trip on a rock along the way. We want to know exactly what will happen and how it will happen and most importantly, we worry about how we'll recover if we fall flat on our asses.

But why would you worry about that, when you don't even know if that will happen?

Why are you so fearful of falling over; why would you plan for tripping?

What if you planned for the success you're going to have on the foggy path? What if you planned for the wins you're gonna have – instead of planning for the fall that you may never come across?

Notice how often we do this, how often we plan for falling and failing. We plan for the absolute worst-case scenario happening and we spend so much time sitting in the space of fear and worry, when it may NEVER happen!

If you're going to cultivate confidence you need to embrace the unknown, the scary "fog of courage." But it doesn't mean you just blindly hope for the best either – no, you have made the choice and decided what your next scary step is, and now you need to feel that fear and allow it to move you.

When you allow the nerves to drive you forward into action (yup, step three is coming) what you're going to find is that all of these 5 Cs work together and end up as one continuous practice.

THIS IS WHAT IT LOOKS LIKE WHEN YOU *DON'T* STEP INTO <u>COURAGE</u>

When you decide not to step into courage there are consequences.

Here are some of the things you could find yourself doing...

YOU'RE ANXIOUS AND OVERWHELMED ♛

When you're constantly worrying about the worst-case scenario happening, you're in high stress and anxiety. You'll find yourself operating from the "flight, fight or freeze" response – and your adrenals and cortisol level will be off the charts! You may recognize this in yourself, if you're constantly worrying about "what will go wrong now?"

The incredible Dr. Joe Dispenza says this about our worst-case scenario tendencies: ***"We spend seventy percent of our lives in stress and survival, anticipating a worst-case scenario based on a past event, and then select the worst outcome and condition our body with fear."***[13]

When you live your life like this, you allow your fearful thoughts and anxious stories to haunt you. When you operate from this space you'll find yourself feeling unsure and insecure, and highly charged with stress.

YOU DON'T TAKE HEALTHY RISKS ♛

You end up doing the mundane, boring, safe, secure things that even you're bored of doing. Life itself is one big risk and although jumping out of an airplane may not be your thing, you need to come to terms with the idea that some things are worth the risk. As the Henry Ford quote says: "If you always do what you've always done, you'll always get what you've always got." And I mean, how boring would that be?!

YOU DAYDREAM, BUT YOU DON'T ACT ♛

You may talk about what you want to do and you may wish for something to happen, but you're not doing anything to make it happen. Wishing and daydreaming will not get you there; at some point in time you need to back yourself and go for it. You'll need to move! Especially if you have big dreams and big goals – the bigger your dreams, the bigger your determination to act on them needs to be.

YOU LIVE WITH RESENTMENT 👑

At the worst end of this scale, you spend your time angry at others and at yourself for not doing what you really want to do. For not following your dreams and for waiting for something to magically happen. Or like I did, you wait for a near-death experience or life-changing moment to wake you up to how precious your life truly is...and how everything you want to create is worth the risk, because your happiness, joy and fulfillment is what's most important.

COURAGE WAS MY ONLY CHOICE

The month of February 2018 was hard. We had a four-month-old baby, a three-year-old son and a mountain of debt. One morning my husband and I looked in each other's eyes and what we saw was fear, scarcity, worry, shame and defeat. We had made some bad financial decisions and now we were faced with some major challenges that required us to be extremely courageous.

We had to step into courage, we didn't have a choice.

I was always the optimistic, positive type (I still am) so in my relationship, I'm always the one rallying: "We'll be fine! We'll get through this!"

But that morning, I felt defeated. For the first time, Hamish saw fear and doubt in my eyes. It was honestly a moment where I felt genuinely scared that I wouldn't know what to do or what action to take to get us out of this mess.

The night that I had decided to leave my job and let go of my styling business a month earlier was only the beginning. There was so much more we needed to do. We sat down and discussed our options so many times and all of them lead to us jumping off the cliff of indecision with no wings.

There was no safety net, no backup plan – nothing. We honestly didn't have the luxury to doubt ourselves.

This business idea needed to work.

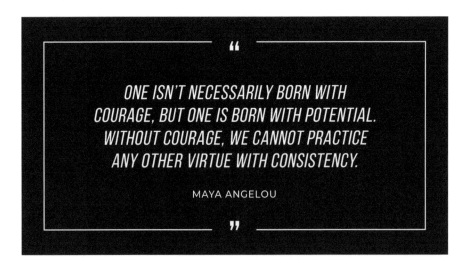

> ONE ISN'T NECESSARILY BORN WITH COURAGE, BUT ONE IS BORN WITH POTENTIAL. WITHOUT COURAGE, WE CANNOT PRACTICE ANY OTHER VIRTUE WITH CONSISTENCY.
>
> MAYA ANGELOU

Although I was terrified, I didn't allow those feelings to hang along for very long. Because I also knew deep down inside that we would find a way to make it work. And that's what we did: we worked so fucking hard that month to keep our lives together.

Hamish started hustling and got the gym back on track and I somehow created a casual role for myself within the same hair and beauty company I'd worked for previously. I was able to work from home (on my own schedule) selling boujee shampoo and conditioner to fancy hair salons around Australia, while breastfeeding my son, and getting this business off the ground.

Most days I was literally breastfeeding while making calls – "So you'll take three bottles of that one and six bottles of this one? You're gonna love it!" – and in between, I was creating content, editing and uploading my videos to YouTube, doing coaching sessions with my clients and planning my confidence masterclasses.

Oh! And I was also playing LEGO with my three-year-old, of course.

The soundtrack to this madness? Gary Vaynerchuk YouTube videos in the background. (Seriously, Gary V was on repeat at my house all day and night – he still is!)

I held my first Creating Confidence masterclass on the 25th of February, 2018. At the end of the masterclass, I offered my coaching services. I was shitting myself, mind you; I didn't know how to sell myself as a coach. I didn't know if I was charging too much or too little. (Spoiler alert – it was definitely too little!)

In other words, I had no idea what the hell I was doing. But I got better every time I tried. At the end of every event I ran (I decided to schedule this same event every month), I signed up new clients and before long, I had a growing list of coaching clients booked in and working with me.

When I made that choice to pursue the goal and build this business, I knew I would be faced with loads of scary decisions – but I made a commitment to myself that I would stand in courage daily, that I wouldn't give up when things felt hard, and that I would put myself out there no matter how awkward or scared I was.

STOP WORRYING
ABOUT FALLING.

We all fall.

IT'S ABOUT HOW YOU GET
BACK UP & NOT MAKE A BIG
DEAL ABOUT THE FALL.

*Just keep
moving.*

ERIKA CRAMER

OVER TO YOU...

Now it's your turn. Where do you need to build some courage? How could you build more courage? How are you going to feel when you're standing in your courage? Are you going to be scared? Are you okay with that? How does that make you feel?

Write it down.

I'll be honest and admit that every time I do something new, I'm shitting my pants with nerves.

But I've reprogrammed the way I see fear: if I feel scared or nervous, it means that I am in the up-leveling stage and that I am on my way to becoming an ever greater, more courageous version of myself.

So here's your **loving bitch slap** if you find yourself here, in step two:

YOU ARE SUPPOSED TO BE SCARED. YOU'RE SUPPOSED TO FEEL THE FEAR – THAT IS COURAGE. KEEP MOVING!

Let go of the idea that courage is some almighty, great and empowering thing. It's not. It feels like shit, it's super scary and when you're creating courage, it means you're probably doubting yourself most of the time! Hello, confidence feels like shit, remember? Well, so does courage!

Take the time to write these questions out and journal your answers – free write with no judgment or limitations:

What does courage look like to you?

How are you going to feel when you're being courageous?

How do you know you're standing in courage?

What do you need to remember when you're right in the thick of creating courage?

What do you want to believe about yourself?

What do you wish for and want for yourself?

Do you want to believe that you're strong? That you can do scary things? Do you want to believe that you're brave and courageous and that you can handle anything that comes your way?

What emotions are you most likely feeling when you're creating the courage you need to do the scary things that matter most to you?

For me: I know I'm being courageous when there are butterflies literally doing handstands in my stomach. I know I feel this way when it's something that's deeply important to me and when I have a lot at risk.

When I feel I am out of my comfort zone, I know that I am in the middle of an up-level.

And I know that on the other side of it, when I've conquered the hard or scary thing, I'm going to feel like a fucking boss. 👑

BREAK IN CASE OF EMERGENCY!

If you feel stuck here, remember this:

YOU ARE SUPPOSED TO BE SCARED. YOU ARE SUPPOSED TO FEEL NERVOUS. THAT IS PART OF THE PROCESS. NO-ONE CAN BYPASS THIS FEELING!

Tell yourself you're excited instead of scared. Your language is very important here.

What words will serve you best: fear or excitement? Nervous or pumped up? Scared or courageous? The language you choose to use here will either empower you to step up, or prompt you to shrink away.

Need more inspiration? Consider this: who do you look up to? Who inspires you? Is there anyone who has gone before you and done the things you want to do? What characteristics of their personality can you take on?

For me it's people like Tony Robbins, Oprah, Gary V – these are all people I look up to in some way, and I take on the characteristics of theirs I love the most.

When you get stuck, who can you look up to to inspire some courage within you?

LATICIA ROLLE

CONFIDENCE FEELS LIKE SH*T

In her words:

"Confidence means having the courage to own every part of your journey, with the ability to step into your power unapologetically. Masks are off and judgments do not exist when one is confident. Confidence is the woman that shines brighter than anyone in the room. Confidence is living in your pure essence, encompassing all of your truths and beauty. Confidence is power.

There are far too many scenarios of when I did not feel confident, but one in particular I would say was the moment I started my business – I had no idea what I was doing designing baseball hats. Whenever I told people about my idea they would look at me confused or crazy; they didn't get it. Their misunderstanding would leave me puzzled and questioning myself.

I was going down an unknown path with little knowledge and I felt small as a woman in business in a male-dominated industry. I lost my confidence along the way of creating my hats, but it didn't stop me from believing in myself. Every time I failed, I turned that into a lesson learned. Eventually when people questioned my design, I would ignore their projections and carry on with my product. In the three years since I launched my product, I've gained the courage to own my "why" – why I created TRESS and trusted my intuition. TRESS is now a thriving online business providing a product for women and men with textured hair, who are confident in who they are.

The key to confidence: persistence and courage."

LATICIA ROLLE
American model, fashion designer and entrepreneur

CHAPTER 8

THE 5 Cs

—

create

W e're half-way through the 5 Cs and we've arrived at **the** most important step. Okay, I feel like I've said this for each step – seriously, it's all so imperative when it comes to practicing confidence. The reason why create is so important, however, is because it's the step that tangibly moves you towards your goals.

Create is about taking aligned, creative action. It's about becoming resourceful and innovative. When you create, the actions you take are in alignment with your choices, your emotions and your feelings.

What you're creating needs to feel good, exciting and inspiring. This is why step three of the practice isn't simply called "action" – anyone can take action. But action just for the sake of action is not useful.

It's not going to change your world.

It's not going to help you live with vitality and purpose.

We live in a world where we're constantly trying to DO something, to hustle hard and be high-achieving action-takers. It seems like we're always taking action towards something. You may find that you get frustrated or even burnt out, and you still don't get the results you want. If this is happening, it's likely because the action you're taking isn't in alignment with what you really want to create. In fact, it is actually counterproductive.

In this step I want to invite you to move away from the idea of just "taking massive action" and doing shit just for the sake of doing it, and I want you to make sure that everything you're doing is aligned to your values.

If it's aligned to your purpose, then this is aligned action taking. I once heard American speaker and spiritual teacher Abraham Hicks[14] speak on this topic. They mentioned that taking one step in aligned purposeful action, is like taking a thousand steps towards that which you want to create for yourself – whereas you could take a thousand (unaligned) actions, and work really hard on the *do-ing*, and still it wouldn't even equate to the impact of that one step you took in aligned action.

Create is a better word than action to explain what you're doing in step three because the truth is, you may not know what the next clear step is. Sometimes, the things you need to do may not be available or obvious to you yet. So – you create it.

You get to create a way to make it happen. You get to create the opportunity. You may have to create a new solution or become resourceful in the way you go about accomplishing something.

And so, while "action" can be very narrow in its meaning, "create" opens your mind to find a different angle, to find a different way, to create an opportunity, create new results – instead of finding reasons why you can't make it happen for yourself.

However, when you create, it allows you the opportunity to innovate and step into your "make it happen" creator vibes.

SMALL STEPS LEAD TO BIG CHANGES

Create is about you making moves towards what you want and taking the small steps required to get there.

Did you hear that?

Yes: THE. SMALL. STEPS.

You see, when you start making empowering choices towards creating confidence and making your dreams a reality, the decisions you make usually feel pretty massive. Meaning, you are usually faced with something big and it can feel really overwhelming when it comes to HOW you're going to actually make it happen.

EP #172

The "how" is actually a number of small actions that will help you conquer the overwhelm. As the phrase says, "How do you eat an elephant? One bite at a time."

Taking small steps toward the big thing you're trying to achieve not only helps you get to the end, but you do so with less stress and more momentum.

The first three steps in the practice of confidence morph into two major moves: choice directly followed by action (courage pops in there quickly to give you a little bit of boldness so the fear doesn't stop you).

One of the biggest mistakes I see my clients make at this point is that they have a massive goal or big vision, and they feel so anxious about how they will ever accomplish it, because they're so focused on the "big-ness" of it all.

Guess what happens when you're overwhelmed and anxious? Nothing. Procrastination and self-doubt kicks in, and the "what if" gremlin ends up at the control panel of your mind.

The most powerful and effective antidote to procrastination is simply to create. All you have to do is take one small aligned action, to make the little move towards the thing you're trying to create.

You want to finally launch your business? Jump on social media and tell your audience.

You want to get fitter and healthier? Join the gym or book a session with the personal trainer.

You want to make better food choices? Go shopping for a shopping cart full of fruit and veggies.

You want to run your first event? Find the venue or book the date in your calendar.

These things may seem small or inconsequential, but what happens when you do these small steps is that they create a snowball effect. You're moving, you're in aligned ACTION, and as long as you commit to moving forward things happen.

Nothing happens when you do nothing – it seems obvious, but when we aren't taking the steps towards the things we want, no wonder we don't achieve the end results!

Say you join the gym and you have a session with your new personal trainer on Monday. You do your first workout and you start to feel energized and excited about this goal to become healthier. This leads you to start thinking about your food choices, which then leads you to clean out your pantry and go food shopping.

You may start walking every morning; you plan out a healthy meal roster. Maybe you add another gym session that week and before you know it, you're feeling fitter!

You have more energy and you're feeling really good about yourself.

These little steps compounded into the result of you being consistent and actually taking repetitive aligned action towards the end goal.

The key to all of this is momentum. We can have *positive* momentum where we are taking small actions towards what we want to create, or we can have negative momentum, where we spiral into inaction and overwhelm – and the overwhelm makes us even more overwhelmed.

The small steps will pay off in the long run and most importantly, they help you build consistency and movement towards what you want.

WHEN YOU
create,
IT ALLOWS YOU THE
opportunity
TO INNOVATE AND
STEP INTO YOUR
"*make it
happen*"
CREATOR VIBES.

— ERIKA CRAMER —

THIS IS WHAT IS LOOKS LIKE WHEN YOU *DON'T* STEP INTO <u>CREATE</u>

When you stop creating, you stop taking action and you end up further away from achieving your goals.

Here are some of the things you may experience:

BURNOUT AND "HUSTLE FATIGUE" ♟

This is the "doing just to do." Taking a bunch of action (as opposed to aligned action) can lead to fatigue, stress and burnout. If you don't have your vision in mind, then why are you "doing" all of the things? This will actually go against what you're trying to create and will leave you feeling like you still have so much to do. It's that "I am always so busy" vibe, when in reality you're not being productive at all.

LOSS OF MOMENTUM ♟

Combined with a lack of energy. This is when your actions aren't paying off. You may have been taking action that lead you nowhere fast, and now you're exhausted and you can't be fucked to take action anymore. You're out of alignment, your energy levels plummet and you may feel like, "What is the point of trying?"

COMPARISON 👑

"Not enough"-ness kicks in here! You look around at everyone's accomplishments or worse, their social media highlights reel, thinking that they've got it all together and you're so far behind in comparison. While you sit there watching (and judging) them, you are actually doing nothing towards reaching your goals.

JEALOUSY 👑

A cousin of comparison, this leaves you feeling sorry for yourself. You indulge in self-pity, loathing and perhaps even anger that they are better off. You wish you could have what they have…

NO GROWTH 👑

And while you're over there coveting someone else's results? Nothing changes for you. The more you watch others and the more you envy the results others have produced, the less *you* do, and the more you judge them and yourself. It's a super unproductive cycle.

LITTLE OR NO RESULTS 👑

Tony Robbins talks about this when he explains our unlimited potential. Basically, when you don't truly believe in yourself, you take little to no action, which gives you little to no results, which then feeds back into your shitty beliefs about yourself that you're not enough…which then leads you to again not take much action. It's another cycle of bullshit that you can avoid by committing to the magic of creation.

Erika is sharing more in her INTERACTIVE book.

See exclusive videos, audios, photos and more...

DOWNLOAD it now at
deanpublishing.com/confidence

A real decision is measured by the fact that you've taken a new action. If there's no action, you haven't truly decided.

– TONY ROBBINS –

OPRAH IS NOT GOING TO COME KNOCKING ON YOUR DOOR

The night I received my shower wisdom message to quit my job and change my side-hustle, was the night my work ethic changed. I had this weird feeling of determination inside of me and I just knew that I had it in me to make this business work. (It was either that, or the fact that we were literally living on the edge financially that was driving me – or maybe both!)

I feel like it was a mixture of: "Holy shit, we HAVE to actually make this happen, there is no Plan B," mixed with my new-found energy and drive, plus a bit of my American grit and resilience. By that point I had lived through so much hardship, I honestly felt like nothing was going to have the ability to break me more than I had already been.

I remember trying to figure out how the hell we would pay our car payment, the rent and other bills. I was so overwhelmed with what to do and I didn't have any clear "aligned" action plans. I called my sister from another mister and long-time mentor, Tanja. When she picked up the phone, I just started sobbing. I was tired from co-sleeping and breastfeeding, I was stressed about the finances and I was in deep beast hustle mode, ready to do whatever it took to get us out of the debt.

She was amazing, and not only because she listened and held space for me to quite literally fall apart. (Sometimes we need a good cry! I swear, something about the salty liquid leaving your eyeballs helps create some much-needed space.)

She was amazing because Tanja had known about our situation, and she was always so great at creating opportunities.

She encouraged me to think about all the ways I could create an income while I was at home with the kids and building my business. After an hour on the phone to her, we had it!

The company I had been working for full-time had a problem. When the sales representatives would go on leave, no one was there to look after the high-level clients. I knew exactly what I could offer them. I recognized their problem and I met them with a solution. We created a casual role that would help them serve their clients while the full-time employees were away, and help me get paid to work from home.

It was brilliant!

This was a game-changer as I was able to continue being with my baby, breastfeed as I needed, serve my hair salon clients AND build my business on the side.

Creating this opportunity made sense to what I was wanting to create for myself. Did I really, truly with all of my heart feel passionate about selling hair products to high-end salons? No.

But if we look at my choice to leave my job and decide to create my coaching business, this action was directly in alignment with that vision.

What would *not* have been an aligned action would have been to just go out and get a job that paid well, but demanded more from me.

The idea here was to CREATE a role for myself and find a way to create the money we needed, while still adding value to the company and to my new business.

Once I did this, I looked at what else I could do. While listening to Gary V's audiobook, I heard him say something that literally changed everything. He said: **no one is going to come knocking at your doors giving you an opportunity – you have to go and create it.**

Mind. Blown.

The whole time I had this crazy subconscious belief that Oprah Winfrey was going to come knocking on my door and say "Hey Erika! I heard you had a hard life? I'd love to help you write a book and get you on television to share your story with the world!" Um, yeah – that was NOT gonna happen.

I realized that I was waiting, hoping, *wishing* that someone would somehow "discover me." It was crazy and one of the biggest **loving bitch slaps** I'd ever experienced.

That's all I needed to hear.

I was committed from that moment onwards to take aligned action in the direction of what I want to create for myself – because no one was going to give it to me.

Needless to say, that very day I started my podcast and recorded my first YouTube video *(if you want to go see this very moment and the story unfold, head to YouTube and search for The Queen of Confidence)*.[15]

That was the moment that The Queen of Confidence coaching business started; Gary V's **loving bitch slap** aligned me into my purpose and drive.

OVER TO YOU...

Are you currently taking aligned action? If not, how can you start to *really commit* to only doing what will lead you to the results you want?

Remind yourself of the decision from step one: what would be the next best thing to do in order to start making that decision, that choice, a reality?

What can you create in order to get you closer to your desired outcome?

I want you to really ask yourself: what's the small step I can take to start moving in the direction I decided on? What's one small, tiny thing you can do? Today? Right now?

If you aren't moving in the direction of your desires then what are you doing? What will it take for you to actually commit to putting what you want first?

Better yet, **HOW** are you going to start doing this?

Get the steps out on paper and get to working on it.

You're not going to be motivated to take action by focusing on the "big" thing. If you do, you'll get stuck. For instance, say you want to lose weight – say it's 25lbs. That's a big, scary, weight loss goal.

How many times a day do you go to the gym? *Zero.* How many times a week do you commit to exercising? *Zero.* So, if you make that choice to get fit and healthy, what's your response to action?

If you're like most people, it will be some version of: "I am **so** committed to this choice to get healthy that I'm gonna go to the gym six days a week, I'm going to exercise for two hours each session and I'm cutting my calories to 800 per day." Um, no girl. No!

This is how we sabotage our success. We sabotage what it is that we want by telling ourselves that it's all or nothing. And if you're going to make a big-ass choice then you need to make a big-ass decision to get some big courage and create big results...

It's not sustainable, or realiztic, and in all likelihood if you go from zero to one hundred like this, you're gonna give up pretty quickly.

Instead: how about you go to the gym twice a week for half an hour?

Or start speed walking around the block or walking the kids to school a couple of times a week? Choose one small thing!

How do you run a marathon?

Step by step, shuffle by shuffle – left foot, right foot, left foot, right foot.

How do you make a million dollars? You make $1, then $50, then $1,000, then $10,000 and so on...You don't go from zero to one million overnight. You make many small steps that eventually compound into something big.

So, what's the next small step you need to make? What are you going to do? Because believe me when I tell you that confidence doesn't get created without your commitment to do something.

Here's your **loving bitch slap** if you find yourself here, in step three:

When we see someone accomplish something big, we can tend to think they are more capable or luckier or more organized than us. But in reality – they are just continuously moving, acting, doing. So many women message me and tell me how I am "killing it" but in reality, I am just taking the actions that align to my vision, every day.

EVERY. DAY. I show up and I work towards what I want. Some days it's crap and there's no momentum. Other days I feel amazing and so productive. *This is the practice.*

EP #6

You don't always feel great, but you show up anyway and the fact that you continue to show up actually pulls you out of your funk. This helps you feel aligned and inspired and builds confidence and momentum to do it all again the next day.

Nothing that you want happens by you sitting on your ass, wishing for it to happen. By doing nothing, playing it safe, hiding and not showing up – you do not get what you want. To add to this, taking action that doesn't align is also not gonna get you far! Being burnt out and exhausted is not going to serve you.

When you lack the energy or motivation to go for your dreams, ask yourself why?

You may be compromising your values and when this happens, you will not feel in alignment. Take some time to really think about what's important to you.

What do YOU value?

Not your parents, not your partner, not what society says – what's actually important to *you*?

Whatever you spend the most time on, that's what you're valuing. If you want to change that, start committing to what you want. Your life, your actions, your outcomes, your results: if you have identified that you're not fulfilled or you're not congruent with your values, you have a massive opportunity here to change it. It takes work, and commitment, but a whole new way of life awaits you on the other side. 👑

FUCK FAKE IT. JUST MAKE IT.

– ERIKA CRAMER –

BREAK IN CASE OF EMERGENCY!

⚡ If you feel overwhelmed by how big your decision is, write it out. Get all the steps you think you'll need to take down on paper. Once you have a list or plan on what actually needs to happen, you can start ticking off the steps you take.

⚡ If you catch yourself going for MASSIVE action or humungous projects and to-do lists, hit pause. Reflect. Is there a way you can break it down even further, make things more achievable, rather than biting off more than you can chew and getting overwhelmed?

⚡ Self-sabotage is one of the most common things we do too, so watch yourself if you're trying to go too big with your actions. One aligned step (no matter how small) after the other is what will create momentum.

⚡ And if you want extra accountability, share your goals, dreams and desires with others. I recently messaged the woman who coordinates the TED Talks in Australia and she recommended I apply. Yup, there's no hiding from that dream now! That one little, tiny action has started the momentum towards me achieving this goal and it will keep me accountable.

⚡ Lastly, remember that one aligned action will lead you to another aligned action, if you stay in alignment and you remain focused on what you want to create. Your movements will become a snowball of momentum: as long as you keep moving forward taking small steps, you'll be on track.

EMMA
ISAACS

CONFIDENCE FEELS LIKE SH*T

In her words:

"I believe we learn a lot when we attempt something we don't yet have the skills for. There's a beauty in the trying and in the attempt, if we can just summon the courage to give our dreams a go. The problem is, we're too attached to outcomes and we forget that the growth is created in the pursuit, and not the result. We're so hung up on getting it right that we often get stuck in inertia – not moving forward – for fear of the failure (that may never eventuate anyway).

What's that quote about not needing to see the whole staircase?

It's true – it's all about taking one step at a time and not overthinking the climb. It's all about perpetual motion. So, if you've got a dream or a goal, try and do one thing every day – whether it's making a phone call or sending an email – that moves you toward that goal. It sounds simplistic because it is. Often, we try and complicate our situations and our decisions but if we just look inward and check in on what we really want, that's where we'll uncover the answers.

This saying also rings true: "If you believe you can, or can't, you're right."

Confidence is about mindset and the quicker we can understand that and work to cultivate more of it, and work on changing the negative self-talk that grips so many of us, the more fulfilled life becomes."

EMMA ISAACS
Founder and global CEO, Business Chicks

I NEVER
LOSE.

I EITHER
WIN
OR I
LEARN.

— NELSON MANDELA —

CHAPTER 9

THE 5 Cs
—
consider

Reflection, evaluation and perspective: that's what our fourth step, consider, is all about.

Once you take the action in step three to *create*, you'll get a result.Now, you need to pause for a moment to consider how that action went.

What was the outcome or the result of the action you took? Every time you take an action (whether it's in alignment or not) you will get feedback on your results. Was it positive? Did you succeed? Did you get the outcome you wanted? Or was the action you took no good? Did you get a shitty result, do you feel like it sucked?

This is where people may say "I failed," but I want you to consider another option here.

Whenever you take an action, whenever you DO something that doesn't work out the way you had imagined it would, you have an opportunity. I personally don't use the word fail and no, it's not because I think it's a bad word. I just believe that words have power.

Your words create your world. Language is so very important, and how you choose to speak about yourself will impact the way you think and feel, especially when you're trying to create confidence. I know that they've tried to make it cool to fail now by saying "fail forward, fail fast." No thank you. It feels very similar to the phrase "fake it till you make it" – and I'd rather say "fuck fake it, just make it!"

In order to arrive at this magical place where you are fully confident and oozing self-belief, you need to redefine what the word "failure" means to you.

If failure to you means you failed and therefore, you're a failure and you haven't succeeded – then I want to invite you to see failure in a different light.

I want you to see failing as *learning*.

If you call it a failure there's going to be shame and all kinds of low vibe energy attached to it, but there doesn't have to be. You *are* gonna fuck some shit up – it's going to happen.

And that's a gift, because it means you get to go back and evaluate what worked and what didn't, so you learn for the next time. You get to take the L – nope, not the LOSS. The LESSON!

If I gave up public speaking because I totally bombed my first gig, I would never be the speaker I am today. But the more I fucked up (what some call fail), the more I LEARNED what I needed to: stop fidgeting, speak slower, take a deep breath before getting on stage, do a power pose…you get me?

When you don't get the result you want (aka you fail) it teaches you something and you get to consider the lesson here. What did you learn? What did that experience teach you?

Maybe you learned that the way you went about that particular action was the wrong way. Now you can attempt it in a different way, so you LEARNED something. It's a lesson – why would you call that a failure?

Think about it: how does it feel when you fail? How does it feel to see yourself as a failure? It sucks and it doesn't feel good at all.

"

IN ORDER TO ARRIVE AT THIS MAGICAL PLACE WHERE YOU ARE FULLY CONFIDENT AND OOZING SELF-BELIEF, YOU NEED TO REDEFINE WHAT THE WORD 'FAILURE' MEANS TO YOU.

"

It doesn't pump you up. It doesn't make you want to go and try again, that's for sure. And guess what? You have to try again every time you fall flat on your ass!

You've got to get your ass back up and go again.

This is how J-Lo, Oprah, Beyonce, and basically everybody who you think is confident does it – this is how they're confident. They fall and they fall hard. They fall publicly. But then? They get their asses back up and they keep it moving, because they got more moves to make, more lessons to be learned. And we can only learn these lessons by messing up and having these difficult experiences.

So, let's say you trip on rock in the fog.

You fall over.

Now you know that you shouldn't walk that way. The next step you take is in a slightly different direction, so you don't make the same mistake again – or you get better at balancing on rocks and not falling over when you step on them.

Every time you fall, every single time that you go the wrong way or you mess up in life, it builds your resilience. It helps you create this unstoppable self-belief within you where you stop caring about the fall.

Where you know you're going to fall or you know there will be times where shit goes wrong, but you don't let that stop you.

Better yet, you get to learn from each and every one of those important experiences.

Welcome to being a human on planet earth!

This statement is true for everyone: I know I am going to fall down, hard. I know people are going to judge me from my fall. I know I'm going to judge myself. I'm going to mess up.

I know this is going to happen. So, I don't stress it. I keep it moving.

And I learn from my mistakes.

After doing this work for so long, I have learned from the times where things didn't go the way I wanted them to go. I have trained myself to go back and to find the lesson. I go back to find the gift, because there's a gift in all of the hard stuff, the shitty experiences, the "bad" times.

There is gold to be mined from each one of those experiences.

THIS IS WHAT IS LOOKS LIKE WHEN YOU *DON'T* <u>CONSIDER</u>

When you don't commit to learning from your experiences, here are some of the things you may be faced with:

YOU TAKE A TRIP TO VICTIMLAND 👑

You remember this hellhole, right? Yup, it's where we are constantly feeling angry, frustrated and taking things personally. It's the place where we have a lack of responsibility and we play the blame game. If you don't start considering your actions and commit to evaluating your results, you will find yourself pointing the finger or making excuses as to why you don't have what you want. You might also become bitter and resentful to others around you who are getting results you want (there's that comparison and jealousy). When you're in this place, you're not thinking clearly and you may make emotional and irrational decisions that keep you even *further* away from the results you're trying to achieve. Stay here too long, and you'll be on your way to becoming a permanent resident of Victimland.

YOU KEEP MAKING THE SAME MISTAKES ♛

When you don't look for the lessons, you can't learn from your mistakes. This leads us to make the same mistakes over and over. These patterns continue to show up until we're willing to look at them and take responsibility for the results we keep getting. Before meeting Hamish, I dated the same guy (different face and name, but same energy) over and over and *over*. I was attracting this same experience to my life, because I wasn't open to changing the way *I was showing up*. This led me time and time again to attract men into my life who were no good for me.

YOU MAKE IT MEAN YOU'RE NO GOOD OR USELESS ♛

If you don't start considering your actions and commit to evaluating how your results go, you will find yourself feeling useless or like a failure. In reality, messing up is completely normal, as educator Jaime Escalante says: "Life is not about how many times you fall down. It's about how many times you get back up." You're actually *supposed* to fall. It's a part of the process. It's part of the growth.

YOU ARE UNABLE TO LEVEL UP OR INNOVATE ♛

When you're not evaluating your results, you're not learning anything new. You end up operating from a fixed mindset instead of a growth mindset. When you look around, all you see are problems instead of opportunities. You can't innovate or solve problems when you're in this lack. Innovation comes from looking at something that's not working well and finding a better way to do it. You won't find a better way until you realize that the current way isn't working – which is why we need to "fail" in order to find a better way to create.

OUR MANY MONEY MISTAKES

The three months that followed my decision to leave my full-time job and start my coaching business were the three months that changed our lives forever. It felt like in that time all we did was learn from ALL the many mistakes we'd made in the five previous years.

When I met Hamish and I started working on myself, we decided that we would invest in growing ourselves personally. This involved us getting credit cards and personal loans, and making some pretty terrible financial decisions.

At the time, we honestly didn't know any better. We just knew that we needed to work on our mindset (I knew I especially needed it, after all the trauma I had been through). Funding it through debt was the only way to pay for it, so that's what we did.

The year before I'd made the decision to start my coaching business, we were living with my in-laws. I was pregnant and the goal was to stay with them for six months so we could save money for our growing family and move out well before the baby was born.

The reality? We ended up there for a year! As I approached the baby's due date I was getting very "nesty," as pregnant women do, and I wanted to move out. Although we had saved up some money, we thought we should rent a house that had more space and was close enough to our in-laws (yes, babysitting!).

But – we made some really bad decisions when it came to moving out. I found a massive place close by that was really high rent (did we really need four-bedrooms?). I was impatient and ready to have this baby, so I didn't care what the cost was. We had planned for a VBAC (vaginal birth after cesarean) at home and not only was I *not* open to having a homebirth at my in-laws, but I also really wanted to create our sacred family space. Who can put a price-tag on the right home to welcome our precious new family member?!

Not me, apparently. We got the house and since it was so big, we bought big furniture. We decked the place out. We also got a new SUV (even though our little car was fine!) because, hello, the crazy pregnant lady was nesting.

So, there we are in our big-ass house with all of our massive furniture and a new SUV. Our savings account was empty. We had a whole bunch of bills coming in. Then Hamish's gym slowed down. Every Christmas this happens – over the silly season, the income dries up. This time, for some reason, we weren't ready for it.

My homebirth? Well, it was magical. Baby Navah made his way into the world at midnight on the 2nd of October. I had a beautiful, peaceful home birth and I met a brand new part of myself. In that birth I was reborn, stronger, calmer, more determined than ever. It was an insanely incredible experience.

Unfortunately once the baby came, the bills came as well. Our stress levels were off the charts and we were in financial problem-solving mode on the daily.

Hamish and I met weekly about our finances. We knew we had made mistakes in the past with our money and were determined to fix them. We set a super tight budget. We stopped eating out, I stopped doing my hair, my nails, my eyebrows and forget about shopping – that was pretty much non-existent.

We looked for a smaller place to live. We sold all of our furniture and we called all of our utilities and credit card companies to ask for payment plans. Shit, we even got a payment plan from the tax department – it was full on!

In summary, in those three months that followed my decision to quit my job and build my business, we had A LOT to unpack and consider. All of the debt we had accumulated was overwhelming, but we learned so much throughout this difficult time.

It taught us responsibility and resilience and most importantly, it taught us that we could overcome this, because we were resourceful. It taught us how to live as minimalists and really be conscious of what we spend money on.

Believe me when I tell you: we needed this experience so badly.

Since we were open to learning from ALL of the many mistakes we had made and we were open to swallowing our pride and asking for help (plus we were happy to work our faces off), it ended up changing our lives for the better.

If we didn't take the time to consider and evaluate our choices here, we would have been destined to repeat those mistakes again and again.

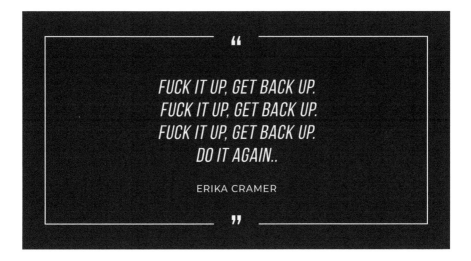

> "
> FUCK IT UP, GET BACK UP.
> FUCK IT UP, GET BACK UP.
> FUCK IT UP, GET BACK UP.
> DO IT AGAIN..
>
> ERIKA CRAMER
> "

Instead, we broke the cycle. And now, we run a million-dollar business. All of the insights from those times have helped us to become better at how we approach financial decisions. We have more money now, but we still don't overspend on things we don't need. We don't use credit cards anymore and if our businesses can't afford it, we don't spend on it.

Today, we live the most minimalist life as that experience taught us about the things that really matter and things that don't.

OVER TO YOU...

So, how did you go? How was that action that you took from step three? When you decided to take the action, how was it? Think of something you just recently did, an action step you recently took.

Can you think back to it and evaluate your result?

What was the outcome? Did you get what you wanted? Are you happy with the result? How can you evaluate whether it was successful or not?

Or did you learn that the action you took wasn't right? Maybe you messed up.

Maybe you dropped the ball at work, or you said something to a girlfriend that you shouldn't have said. Okay, so you made a mistake. What did that experience teach you? What happened? Where do you think you went wrong? Why? If you had to do it again, what would or could you do differently?

This step, consider, is all about you becoming the Sherlock Holmes of your life. You can go back to the situation and extract the good, extract the lessons from every time you "fail."

Here's your **loving bitch slap** if you find yourself here, in step four:

THIS IS A PART OF THE PROCESS! YOU WILL FUCK IT UP!

Learn from it! It is not a failure. You are not a failure.

Your mantra from now is: fuck it up, get back up, fuck it up, get back up.

Hamish and I made some super shitty financial mistakes in our past. And guess what?! Next time we will make smarter decisions. As Maya Angelou says, "When you know better, you do better."

Consider the fact that you and everyone else you meet is doing the best they can with what they know. If you don't mess shit up, you don't get the chance to know better. It's as simple as that. Dust yourself off and keep it moving, shorty! 👑

YOU'RE NOT GONNA KNOW.

Choose, live,

IF IT WORKS OUT GREAT AND IF IT DOESN'T

Adjust.

— GARY VAYNERCHUK —

BREAK IN CASE OF EMERGENCY!

You're always fine-tuning and learning. This is the core principle of the practice of confidence.

Repeat after me: I will fuck all this up. I will most definitely forget everything Erika is telling me to do. And, that's okay.

Not only is it okay – it's normal!

More importantly: with the practice of the 5 Cs, you'll start to see that fucking up and getting back up again is all just part of life, sister. The aim of the game isn't to stop messing up – it's to stop beating yourself up about it when you do.

So when you take an action, be willing to evaluate and consider: "How was that? Did I get the result that I wanted?"

If not, thank you! Lesson learned.

If yes, thank you! Outcome achieved.

Either way, thank you! Now you know what you don't want. Now you know how you need to show up. Now you can focus on what your next move is.

With step four, every time you take action and you put yourself out there and you do that scary-ass thing that you mustered up the courage to go for – stop and ask yourself, what did I learn from that? What did that teach me?

Take that lesson and move it into the next time you do it again. DO NOT LET THAT STOP YOU!

Remember: you will mess up. You will forget ALL this shit I'm telling you.

You'll fuck it up. Fuck it up. Get back up! Get. Back. Up!

It's not only human to mess up, it's expected. There was once a time when you didn't know how to walk, or drive, or tie your shoelaces. I mean we learn how to do all kinds of things that we never knew how to do. You gotta give yourself that chance.

So step four, consider, did you really fail?

Did you really suck?

Did you make a mistake or did you learn that the way you didthat specific thing didn't work and now you have some insight into how you can make your next move?

How good is that?

How amazing!

Thank you, failures.Thank you, mistakes. Now I get to be better.

SOPHIE
WILLIAMS

"I think about myself when I was younger, in my early 20s, and I can't believe how unconfident I was. It's like I was a different person. Life seemed very big and scary and I used to feel like things would happen to me, rather than me being in control.

I think that all started to change for me when I learned to say no, to put my boundaries in place. It's not always easy to do, and in the beginning it can feel almost impossible – telling people who expect you to be one thing, or one way, that you've grown and changed. But it's so essential.

Now, if anything, I'm too confident!

My favorite thing about that is it's given me the security to admit when I've done something wrong, and when something is my fault. In the past, I would have been too embarrassed, or scared of looking stupid, and I would have tried to hide my mistakes, but now I'm happy to hold my hands up and say "I fucked up, I'm sorry – let me try to fix this."

I've also been able to use my confidence to speak up as an advocate for other people, which has been the greatest thing I've learned as I've got older – using my confidence to be a good ally."

SOPHIE WILLIAMS
Author and anti-racism activist in the UK

CHAPTER 10

THE 5 Cs

—

continue

This is all about momentum, baby! Step five is continue, where it all comes together: it's the "snowball stage" of the practice.

This is also the step that connects right back into step one, choice. You see, when you're *living and breathing* the 5 Cs, then this step (continue) becomes a way of life.

It means you are committed to always going back to step one and choosing what's next, into step two to get that courage going, into step three to create the aligned action, into step four to consider your results, you evaluate, reflect and then boom! Continue – YOU. DO. IT. ALL. AGAIN.

AND AGAIN.

AND AGAIN.

You keep it moving, that's the practice – it actually becomes one continuous movement. It happens so fast sometimes that you may not even know what step you're on. And that's why I've slowed it down and broken it into bite-sized steps for you, now you know what to do if you get stuck. You know what your next "C" is.

The idea with this practice is that you don't stop moving through it; remember like the commitment to meditation, there is no "arriving" at a final destination. With the 5 Cs, it's the practice itself that gets you creating confidence. If you stop, you're not in the practice anymore. So guess what? You're not gonna get better at it.

You're not going to cultivate and create confidence.

When you stop, you're no longer in creation mode. The more you continue to move forward with these five steps, the more you don't even realize that you're in a step. Continuing becomes a way of life and it keeps you in the practice of confidence, always and forever.

Why? Because it's called growth. Hopefully by now you've got your head around the idea that you will not get to a final place. You will never achieve "confident," you'll be doing confident things. You'll be doing things that confident people do, which is making choices and decisions, mustering up some fucking courage when really you're scared as hell, putting yourself out there with your actions and evaluating how it all went so that you can do it all again.

Can you see how it's a practice with no end-point? You'll always have to make another choice, get encouraged for the next scary thing, so you can take action to then ask yourself, "How was that? Okay, maybe it was shit. Let's try that again..." or "That was amazing! I got this, let me keep this momentum going!"

Whether it's good, bad, or needs work, you are there showing up, and making it happen for yourself.

Continue is about being committed to moving, growing and evolving. If you stop, you don't grow. If you stop, you don't create. If you stop, you don't keep making choices and decisions don't get made in your life (or at least not the ones you want to be making). There's no courage being created in your world.

There's no alignment and no action being taken, no small steps towards the things that you want.

> CONTINUING BECOMES A WAY OF LIFE
> AND IT KEEPS YOU IN THE PRACTICE
> OF CONFIDENCE, ALWAYS AND FOREVER.

So then, you don't get what you want.

And what's worse, you may start to think, "Oh, it's because I'm not good enough."

Nope! Wrong. It's because you didn't continue to move, it's because you stopped moving.

There's no such thing as being "wrong" or "failing" and it's ridiculous to judge ourselves as "not enough" just because we made a mistake.

Maybe you needed to make that mistake? Maybe you needed to learn something. I can almost guarantee that there was a lesson you needed to experience.

So, there is no end with the 5 Cs. There is no: "Yasss! I'm there. I've made it!" There's no "making it." It's called life. It's called growth.

You get better each and every time you try and that's the whole point – when you're in the practice of confidence, you get to keep evolving into a greater, more aligned version of yourself.

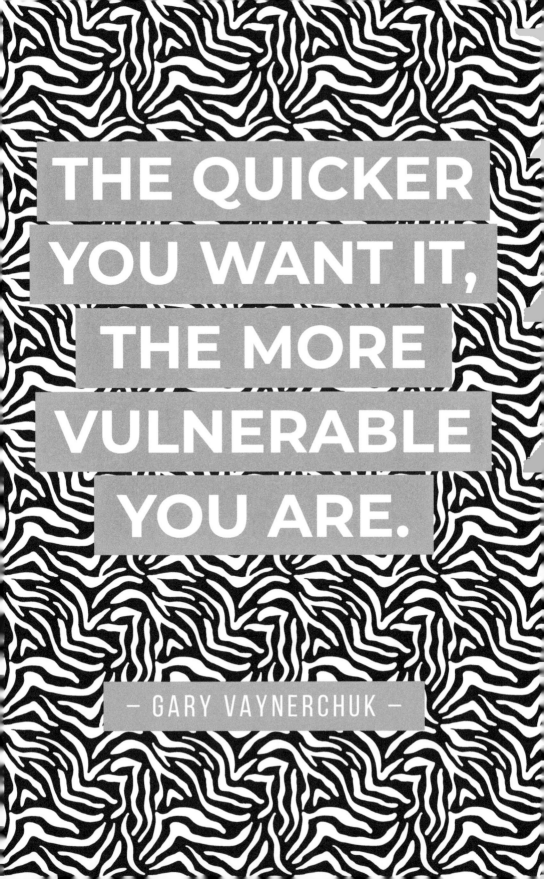

THE QUICKER YOU WANT IT, THE MORE VULNERABLE YOU ARE.

— GARY VAYNERCHUK —

THIS IS WHAT IS LOOKS LIKE WHEN YOU *DON'T* STEP INTO <u>CONTINUE</u>

Here are some of the things you may experience when you stop at step five in the practice:

BASICALLY, EVERYTHING FROM STEP ONE 👑

I'm serious. When you stop moving forward because you got it wrong or you messed up, what do you think happens? You sit in self-doubt. You make it mean that you're "not good enough." You sit in self-pity. You go visit your pity party peeps in Victimland. What happens is that you give up, you lose momentum and then? Nothing. Nothing happens for you. You get no closer to your goals or your dreams, because you stopped moving towards them. It's simple. If you move, you get closer. If you stop, you don't. I know this shit isn't rocket science my love BUT it is powerful. Think of a time when you messed up and felt *so bad* about it that you decided to hide, or stop showing up, stop speaking out, stop putting your hand up, stop sharing your feelings, stop trying to connect, stop dating or posting on social media? Then what happened? Nothing. Am I right? You stopped. Then time passed by. Then because so much time went by with you doing nothing, you started to doubt yourself (even more). Now more time has passed, still no movement in the direction of what you want to achieve or create…(which feels even shittier). More time plus no movement equals even more self-doubt, guilt, self-pity and comparison. The more you stop moving, the more that nothing happens. So, you watch and wait and judge and wait and feel bad because now, there's been A LOT of time passing. **The bigger the gap, the more that SELF-DOUBT has the ability to creep in like a crow bar, intervening into your practice of confidence.** So, don't stop moving. Even if you can't run anymore, fucking shuffle – get one foot in front of the other. Whatever you do, please do not stop moving.

FROM CAN'T BUY BREAD TO BANKING SIX FIGURES

So, you may be wondering how Hamish and I went from struggling to buy bread, stressing to pay our electricity bill and looking for coins under the seat, to making six figures per year and not having to worry about money?

Don't worry sister, I got your back. I'm an open book. I'm going to let you in on the secret.

Are you ready? Okay, here it is. So, what happened is…

I didn't stop moving. I worked my ass off. I fell over many times but got back up even more times.

I lived and breathed this practice. To this day, I am in it.

The 5 Cs is how I live my life.

Early 2018 was "struggle town" for the Cramers. There were so many hard moments and decisions, big and small, that I agonized over. I chose to write out every single decision we had to make (and I still do – writing and getting the thoughts out of your head and onto paper is such a powerful way to get clarity).

To be honest, courage **had** to come to us, because we didn't have the luxury of doubting ourselves. I couldn't sit in my comfort zone.

It was either **show up** or be broke as a joke, beg my in-laws for money or create even more credit card debt and be miserable as hell.

I was not about to do *any of that*.

I needed to dig deep into my resilience and my determination. I needed to go beyond myself and really find my "why."

Why was I doing all of this? How much did leaving a legacy and helping women mean to me? (Turns out, A LOT!)

Was I really going to be able to make an impact on women around the world if I went all in? Was my happiness worth all of this struggle and hard work?

Fuck yes it was.

I am so grateful that we got pushed up against the wall during that time; that we had to go through that horrible, difficult experience. Because if we didn't, and I stayed in my perfectly safe comfort zone or my okay job. I may still be sitting around "wishing" I could change the world and "one day" be the female Tony Robbins, waiting for Oprah to come knocking at my door.

Maybe, it was all meant to happen the way it did.

Would I do it again? HELLS to the yes! All of it – in a heartbeat.

The mistakes, the ridiculous choices that led to massive amounts of debt, the stress, the tears and the hard work – I would take that *any* day over living an unfulfilled, miserable life.

Think about all the people you know who aren't happy.

Who don't have the relationships they want to have, who don't ever make the money they wish they could, who don't have their health, who don't work in jobs that light them up, who don't live where they wish they could...

So many people live this way, as if it's normal to hate your life?!

I mean, do we really need to end up at a family funeral or have our best friend be told she has cancer for us to actually realize how fucking precious our very existence is?

Do we really need a near-death or dramatic experience to wake us up to our life?

Why aren't we creating the life we want to experience?

What are we really waiting for?

Is it permission?!

Do you need permission to go for the life you want?

Do you need permission to truly be happy?

Okay!

Go on and give it to yourself then:

IT'S NOT "CAN YOU."

IT'S "WILL YOU."

ERIKA CRAMER

Permission Slip

_____

♛ You have permission to show up.

♛ You have permission to take up space.

♛ You have permission to change your mind.

♛ You have permission to put yourself first.

♛ You have permission to piss your family off, if it means making yourself happy.

♛ You have permission to love yourself.

♛ You have permission to love your body.

♛ You have permission to accept yourself as you are.

♛ You have permission to know that you are perfectly imperfect and that is fucking fabulous.

♛ You have permission to say no.

♛ You have permission to do what the fuck YOU want to do with your life.

♛ You have permission to be who the fuck you are in this moment.

_____

(Signed by: YOU, the only person you ever really need permission from.)

OVER TO YOU...

I want you to think about your life right now. If you had to choose, from step one to step five, where are you currently at, where would you place yourself? Where have you gotten stuck in the practice of confidence?

Take this time to really look at your life right now – not yesterday, not next week, but right now, in this moment.

Where are you in the practice *today*?

Are you in step one: *choice*? Do you need to make a choice, a decision that you know you haven't made?

Or are you in step two: *courage*? Are you scared as hell? Do you need to start moving and actually do the scary thing that you're so worried about? Can you feel the pee dripping down your leg or is there a butterfly party in your stomach and you feel scared to take the next step?

Maybe you're in step three: *create*, and you're ready to take some aligned action. Do you need to start taking small steps in the direction of where you want to go?

Or did you already take the action? How was it? Are you in step four: *consider*? Was it a great result that brought you momentum? Or did you mess up, fall over and learn that the action you took wasn't quite right?

Or do you find yourself here in step five: *continue*? Are you feeling flat or purposeless? Do you feel shame for not moving forward? (P.S. It's never too late to keep moving.)

Where are you right now, one to five?

Have a think about it, then write it down.

Which step have you gotten stuck at and what is your next move?

If I get stuck in my head, where I'm thinking "what if this" or "what if that" and I'm in self-sabotage, procrastination or overwhelm, I know that I am in **choice** and I have decisions to make.

If I find myself in fear, in worry or feeling scared of the worst-case scenario, then I know for sure that I am in **courage** and that's my next step.

When there's no momentum, I am not in alignment and I am not getting the results I want, I know I am not creating. Taking aligned action to **create** is my next move.

If I find myself sad, upset, angry, feeling sorry for myself or lacking major confidence and self-worth, then I am in **consider** and I need to make time to sit with my results.

When I feel flat and purposeless and I feel like nothing's going on in my world, then I haven't continued. I haven't gone back to the next thing that I want to create for myself. I haven't gone back to actively choosing. Sometimes, it's because I haven't allowed myself the time and space to process my feelings or I may be choosing to numb out.

If I am here, I know that I've stopped at **continue**. (When I lost my husband, I felt like I lived in this blank space for five years straight.)

There are things in each step that are going to get in the way; it's not always a straight, linear path forward. You need to recognize when this happens so you can take the next step – because there is ALWAYS another step forward that you can take.

Here's your **loving bitch slap** if you find yourself here, in step five:

Don't stop moving. Don't let yourself lose the momentum. The longer you stop for, the more you doubt yourself. The more you doubt, the less action you take. This is a breeding ground for second-guessing yourself, seeking permission, hiding and not taking up your space.

If this goes on for too long, the very length of your own inaction will stop you from moving and making choices.

DON'T STOP MOVING.

Just go back to step one and make a choice. Decide what you're going to do and get to doing it. 👑

BREAK IN CASE OF EMERGENCY!

THIS IS VERY IMPORTANT.

Sometimes when you take an action and consider how you went (step four) you may find yourself feeling all the feels. You may be upset with the end result you got, you may have to process what comes up for you and at times it may be a whole lotta emotion.

I am not going to pretend that you should just "get on with it" and take action anyway – NO WAY. That's not helpful at all. Instead, only you'll know what you need, so be sure to give it to yourself.

I know for myself when I mess up and shit doesn't go to plan, I need a minute to regroup, to check in with how I am feeling. I am a super communicator so I find expressing myself (usually to my amazing husband) helps me create some space. Sometimes I need to have a shower and massive cry or scream into a pillow. Basically, I need to do something for myself to process the experience, especially if the results I got were not what I wanted.

So, I want to leave you with this extremely useful and actionable checklist on what to do if this happens to you.

I want to teach you a simple and very powerful way to "coach yourself." (So you basically have me living in this book as your hype woman when you find yourself in a funk, yay!)

EP #160

THE 7 STEPS TO COACHING YOURSELF

STEP ONE: CHECK YOURSELF

First and foremost, check in: how are you feeling? What's going on for you? Becoming aware of what's coming up for you is key to shifting your vibe and your state. How is your energy right now? Then ask yourself "What do I need right now?"

STEP TWO: JOURNAL IT OUT

Journaling always helps me find out what's REALLY going on, it helps me unpack and unravel how I feel and why. Here are some prompts as a reminder from pages 83-84. How do I feel right now? What am I currently thinking? Why do I feel like this? (Asking why is a great way to get to the core of that's going on).

STEP THREE: CALL A TIME-OUT

Taking the time you need is everything. This allows you to not become reactive in the moment. Remember when your emotions are high your intelligence is low (meaning you don't make logical decisions). Take the time you need to center yourself and don't make any major decisions until you're in a better mind space.

STEP FOUR: CRY

Cry! And then cry some more. Here's the truth – we don't cry enough and when we do, we fucking apologize for it! (Can you please stop doing that?!) Crying is such a deep release that we all need more of. Don't judge yourself here or try to figure out a reason "why" you're crying, just let yourself cry. Let that salty liquid come out of your eyeballs and don't make it mean shit.

STEP FIVE: SHAKE IT OFF

Now it's time to "change your state," as the amazing Tony Robbins says. The fastest way to shift how you feel emotionally is to shift your body physically. Jump, do some pushups, go for a run, DANCE! (Pump them tunes up loud!) Do some breathwork or have a cold shower. Shaking your body up has been proven to drastically change your mood and your energy levels.

STEP SIX: LET IT GO

You may have gotten into a funk or spiraled into a crappy mood but now you need to let it go. It happened, you got the lessons from it (hopefully) so stop bringing it back up. Catch yourself if you try to bring up the past again, or call your friends about it and relive the moment that got you into the shitty funk in the first place. It's not helpful and it's over so LET. IT. GO. YO!

STEP SEVEN: CREATE A CONFIDENCE MINDSET

Commit to growing and expanding yourself. Commit to pushing yourself out of your comfort zone on the daily. Your mindset is the key to creating everything you want in your life. Here are some things you can do to up-level your mindset: Listen to podcasts that educate, empower and challenge you to think differently. Read more books on mindset or something you want to learn (or listen to audio books). Hire a coach, a mentor or jump into a community or program of like-minded people who can uplift you and help hold you accountable to creating what you want. Bend the corner of these pages or stick a bookmark in it, I can almost guarantee you'll want to revisit this checklist time and time again sister.

thequeenofconfidence.com/how-to-coach-yourself[16]

STOP WORRYING ABOUT GETTING IT 'RIGHT'...

JUST GET IT.

ERIKA CRAMER

LISA
MESSENGER

CONFIDENCE FEELS LIKE SH*T

In her words:

"What does confidence mean to me? It's feeling happy, grounded, strong, resilient. Have an unwavering self-belief. Knowing that I can do anything I put my mind to. And truly anything is absolutely possible.

I have a number of rituals, routines and disciplines in my well-honed toolkit that I draw on every day, particularly if something happens to make me feel less confident. Firstly, I let myself feel the feeling. I think rather than brushing it away and trying to diminish it, it's really important to feel it and then face it. Then I remove myself from the feeling and try to look in at it to question where it is coming from, what the trigger is, what the underlying root cause of it is?

Once I understand the feeling and its cause, I can then take steps to conquer it. More often than not in my experience, feelings associated with low self-esteem, lack of self-worth or low confidence are habitual and if we can learn them, we can unlearn them. I take a deep breath and then feel into all the reasons why I am good enough. Why I can step up. It takes effort and work and the ability to get comfortable being uncomfortable, but when you take a little risk to believe in yourself, the ordinary can become extraordinary or the impossible – possible."

LISA MESSENGER
Founder and editor, Collective Hub; author, speaker and entrepreneur

THE PRACTICE
OF CONFIDENCE
(FIVE Cs)

1. CHOICE

This is all about decision making. We all have choices we can make. So: what's the one decision you need to make right now?

TIP: Don't let fear get in your way – what would you love to do? Think big.

2. COURAGE

This is about knowing that confidence doesn't always feel good, it's hard work. You gotta push through the discomfort (making you courageously uncomfortable). Confidence does take courage. How are you willing to show up?

TIP: Confidence is your ability to take action while you are shitting yourself. Everyone is scared, act anyways.

My **#lovingbitchslap** reminders to you:

- ♕ No one is confident, it's a practice that takes commitment, you gotta do the work!
- ♕ Stop telling yourself you're not confident. You will never have it if you keep telling yourself you lack it. Watch your words.
- ♕ Decide to show up and take action immediately. No more self-sabotage – GET MOVING!

3. CREATE

What's the ONE thing you need to act on? The first step to get you started?

TIP: Don't get stuck in overwhelm. I am suggesting one small step. Small steps create momentum and consistency, which will get you moving forward. Action is your way through sista!

4. CONSIDER

What came as a RESULT of your ACTION? How did you go in the action step?

TIP: Consider you can't fail, you will only learn. You may learn that it didn't work out. Why? What did this teach you for the next time? Your results are a reflection of this practice so take a moment to consider what you learned.

5. CONTINUE

Do it all again. Forever. And ever. What's your next decision? Action?

TIP: Confidence is a practice. One you commit to daily, hourly, sometimes even moment to moment. You must CREATE your confidence.

Your dreams
DON'T HAVE TO
BE BIG.

THEY HAVE TO BE
Yours.

— GARY VAYNERCHUK —

CHAPTER 11

YOUR
CALL TO
confidence

Here we are, near the end of the book. And now? Now, it's really over to you.

Because what comes next for you is completely up to you.

Sounds scary, I know. But you got this, sis. The fact that you picked this book up in the first place was the first step you took towards becoming more confident. **And I want to acknowledge you**.

I want to acknowledge you for reading and for finishing this book, for being open to thinking in different ways and for allowing me to guide you on this journey of creating your confidence. I acknowledge you for experiencing the questions, exercises and stories in this book. And if you've read this far, I can bet that you've already started to reframe your mind around how you want to think, who you want to be and what you want to create for yourself.

By now, you probably know why I've decided to call this book *Confidence Feels Like Shit*. Everything we've covered together represents some of the hardest and most important work you'll ever do on yourself.

You've learned about the importance of managing your mind and questioning your thoughts. You discovered about how truly important it is that you #FWOT and let people think whatever they're going to think about you. By now you have an understanding of how to stop people pleasing, the power of saying no, letting go of the pursuit of perfection and constant comparison. Last and definitely not least, you've learned the steps to finally start creating your confidence on the daily (no matter where you're starting from).

You've made your way through the 5 Cs and learned about the power of consistency and momentum, plus how to coach yourself whenever you find yourself in a funk. (Damn look at you girl, I hope you're proud of yourself!) But the work doesn't end here – actually, here is where it starts.

All of this information is cool but in reality, it's all a bunch of words on pages in a pink book. It doesn't actually make a difference what you just read through if you're not gonna actually apply this information.

Information can be really useless if you do nothing with it. We live in an era where there is an information overload, where you can literally Google or YouTube anything you want to know. So in reality, it's not about the information you got, it's about the application.

Are you going to actually DO something with the information I've shared in this book?

Even if all you read was Chapter One and you actually applied the concepts there (for example, the one about having the Ability – to – Respond) your life could change forever.

This is why I tell my clients to stop "binging," to stop seeking more information and sometimes to stop consuming altogether, because there is such a thing as information overload. As Tony Robbins so powerfully says: *"You see, in life, lots of people know what to do, but few actually do what they know."*[17]

Imagine if you **knew** that your life could be changed forever, if you actually put what you learned in this book to practice?

Would you waste another day?

THE MOMENT THAT CHANGED ME FOREVER

The 19th of June 2013 was the day that broke me.

Three days earlier, I was celebrating my 30th birthday. The night of my birthday, Hamish and I were due to fly to Indonesia for our first ever retreat. Little did I know that this retreat would be my rebirth, my initiation.

Seven years after Jeo's death, I was about to experience the biggest transformation of my life; but not before walking through the flames and going through the biggest emotional breakdown I've ever had. Hamish and I had only started dating nine months prior and our journey so far had taken us knee-deep into personal and business development.

At this point, we had discussed our future and we both knew we wanted to be together forever. We spoke about getting engaged, then married. When the opportunity to go to this retreat came up, I had told Hamish that I really wanted us to go. I knew that I needed this shake up and I was ready to go deep within myself. Hamish was excited as well, but as always, was way more practical than me.

"Babe, this thing costs $8,000 – which is how much I was going to spend on your engagement ring," he said. "If we go to this retreat we're not going to have anything left." Me being me, I said "Babe, fuck that! I don't need an $8,000 ring.

I need this retreat! I need this experience – WE need this experience."

That is a moment we still look back on. The moment we bet on **ourselves**. We went all in and we bet on ourselves.

A retreat in Bali sounds fun, right? Relaxing? Maybe some yoga, a healthy menu, an afternoon massage and an evening meditation?

This was NOT that kind of retreat. Not by a long shot.

Which is why, just two days after arriving at the retreat, I was sitting in the conference room of the Club Med resort, crying so hard that I thought my head was going to explode. I could barely breathe.

I was having an emotional breakdown.

I had reached my breaking point and I knew that this had to happen then and there. This was my moment of truth; I went all in with my emotions. It was messy and it was painful but holy fuck, it changed me and set my life in a completely different direction.

But, like, hold up: in the moment, it was horrible.

It wasn't pretty and it was so damn uncomfortable to be in, because I was on the verge of my biggest ever breakthrough. We had flown all the way to Bali for this retreat. We had spent all of our savings to get there.

And a big part of me was thinking: we flew all this way and spent all this money to have a fucking mental breakdown in paradise?

WTF?!

> ## I KNEW THAT THIS WAS EITHER WHERE I WOULD WASTE ALL OF OUR MONEY BECAUSE IT WAS ALL FOR NOTHING...OR, MY LIFE WOULD CHANGE FOR THE BETTER, FOREVER.

Weirdly enough, I kind of knew that would happen. I mean, we left our (secure, familiar and comfortable) home to fly to another country, to be in an environment where everything is new and unknown and where you're purposefully there to heal, to unravel yourself and to work on all the parts of you (you cannot hide when you go on these kind of retreats).

There I was at my lowest low, and in that moment, I knew that this was either where I would waste all of our money because it was all for nothing…or, my life would change for the better, forever.

So what went down? Here goes…

That morning, our mentor asked us to do an exercise. *Please know that I did this exercise in a supervised environment with the right people who could guide me, so please don't go trying to fuck yourself up with this at home!*

He asked us to imagine our current reality, what we had been doing up to that point. How we were living and getting the results we didn't want.

How we were self-sabotaging, lacking confidence, lacking self-belief and really just not going for what we wanted like our lives depended on it.

He painted us the picture of the day when we would have to leave the earth, the day where our physical bodies are no longer here, the day we transition and our life ends.

He said: "Imagine nothing changes and you keep doing what you're doing now. Imagine you keep going through your life the exact same way you are now – not having the results you want, wishing and hoping for more, but never getting it. Not living the life you want to live, not finding love, not being happy, not leaving a legacy for your family, not leaving the world a better place, not hitting your potential…"

Oof. This shit was hitting home for me.

Next he said: "Imagine the person who loves you the most in the world has to get up and speak at your funeral. They have to read your eulogy...what would they say? Who would be up there sharing about the life you wish you had, but never got the chance to create?"

Although it sounds full-on and a bit exaggerated to do this, at the time, in this retreat, in this safe container that we were in – this exercise was the push that gave me my moment of truth.

Fuck. I was ruined. I couldn't even fathom.

Instantly, my mother's face popped into my head. I was all my mother had. She never married anyone and she didn't have any other children, plus her family had always been pretty estranged and distant.

I had lived most of my life (from 17 years of age) thousands of miles away from her.

And although I didn't have any guilt for moving away and living my life, all of a sudden, the thought of her speaking at my funeral brought so much guilt and pain into my body.

I imagined her heartbroken to know that her daughter was gone too soon. I imagined that she would feel so alone.

I instantly started writing so fast and so intensely that I could barely read what I was writing. The pages filled with drops of water, my tears that, by this point, were pouring down my face.

It was so hard to write, so hard to imagine myself in that position as my mother.

I am positive that I didn't really write what she would have written or said but at the time, the exercise was about you yourself having the opportunity to be faced with this reality, pretending you could know somehow what that person would say about your life.

Doing this exercise, I saw that I didn't get to live my life the way I had always thought I would – I never got to become the person I knew deep inside I wanted to become. I didn't get to achieve all the dreams and massive goals I had of changing the world in my own way, of helping others, of becoming a mother...I didn't get the chance to do anything that I really wanted to.

The flashbacks of the life I had lived up to this point came flooding in. My childhood, the Army, my back accident, losing Jeo, being in Australia on my own, not having any family, still not having much money, still struggling with my self-worth and my confidence...

Erika was my only daughter, and she was an incredible daughter. She was always so helpful and caring of others, and she really wanted to change the world. It's unfortunate that she didn't get the chance to do everything she dreamed of. She didn't even scratch the surface of her potential. She had so much to give and so much to do. She was gone too soon. She had so many dreams and goals. If she would have believed in herself and not allowed her fear or her shame to hold her back, I just know she would have gone so far. She could have changed the world. Erika went through all of that trauma and hardship only to suffer... I wish I could have had one last chance to tell her how amazing she was. To remind her of how important and worthy she was. She was supposed to heal her pain, she knew better than to doubt herself, why did she constantly doubt herself? Why did she allow her past experiences to keep her in fear? Why did she think so small of herself? Did she not know how brilliant she was and how amazing she was? She could have done more. I should have done more. She could have done it all, she didn't get to do what she wanted. Erika had so much more to give this world…

My hands were shaking and my vision was blurry from all the tears that filled my eyes. My paper was drenched with tears and I had never felt so much pain in my heart. I was broken at that moment, overwhelmed with grief, sorrow and regret.

I sobbed so hard that it hurt my chest and sent a throbbing ache to my temples. I was fucked. It was horrible. Gut-wrenching. He sent us all on a break. I couldn't speak or make eye contact with anyone on the break. I didn't even speak to Hamish. I was in such a fucked up, dark place.

He left us there to reflect for about an hour. When we came back in the room, he gave us an opportunity to rewrite our story. No one spoke; we all sat back and you could have heard a pin drop as he explained the next part of the exercise.

"Thankfully, you have an opportunity here today to decide how your life will turn out. You have an opportunity right now to change your life for the better," he said.

"Thankfully that exercise was only an exercise – and you're still here, living and breathing. You get another chance to create the life you want. You get a chance to choose how your life turns out…"

I closed my eyes as I listened to him speak.

I wanted to feel every part of the second chance I was about to get to create my future.

He continued: "So, how do you want it to turn out? What do you want to create, what do you want your life to look like?

What is the legacy you wish to leave behind for yourself, for your family, for the world?

How do you want it to be told?"

I breathed a deep, deep sigh of relief and I opened my eyes. It was such a crazy moment for me. It was like this beast mode moment – this inner fire had been ignited inside me, and I started writing again furiously and intentionally.

In that moment, as crazy as it sounds, I was reborn.

It was THE moment that everything changed for me.

I was still sobbing hard, yet this letter had a different energy to it: it was full of determination, of a matter-of-factness, a drive to change.

My daughter Erika lived an incredible life.

She inspired me every day with her determination and her willingness to never give up on herself or others. She cared so deeply about helping others that she dedicated her whole life to it.

She led women from all over the world to truly believing in themselves. She wrote books, she spoke to millions of people and she achieved her dreams of becoming an influential woman around the world. She met Oprah and spoke on stage with Tony Robbins, she worked with every single one of her mentors and she helped create opportunities for others to do the same. She was so loving and friendly and built a connected community of incredible followers and friends around the globe.

She loved to travel; she even came back to her hometown and spoke to the foster kids. She was so passionate about inspiring other kids like her and she donated millions to fund programs for them to keep them off the streets and in school.

She even got a chance to perform and act; she always loved that. She lived a full life and she was an incredible mother.

I am so blessed to have seen my daughter become the woman she did and her children now have so many memories of her to look back on, her shows, her videos, her interviews and books, that's who she was. She never forgot about me and she flew me everywhere she went. I had so many beautiful experiences with my daughter, she made me so very proud.

She left her legacy and inspiration for all to follow and Erika continues to inspire me daily. My daughter lived her life to the fullest and she will continue to live on, inside every single person who she touched with her life and message."

Fuck! There I was again, sobbing my heart out.

But this time, I had this insane energy inside of me – my hands were vibrating. It was almost too much to take it in. I have never ever, until this day, felt that level of DETERMINATION and focus for my life.

It was next level.

It was that very moment that the Queen of Confidence really was born (even though I was styling then), because that was the moment that I decided I would stop playing small, I'd stop doubting myself, and I would get to making my dreams a reality.

You have an opportunity right now, just like I did at that retreat in Bali, to change how your story ends up.

So this is my invitation, my final **loving bitch slap** to wake you up to your potential.

I don't want you to just tell yourself some bullshit in your mind. "Yeah, wow, I get it Erika. I need to show up, practice confidence… yeah, I know what you mean."

Then you put this book down, go back to your life and your normal habits and…nothing changes.

No! No way. You know better than this now.

And knowing means you are actively DOING it; knowing is getting the results in your life.

Here's the good news: this book isn't "done." I hope that you live and breathe this book – or as I say to my clients "don't read the book, BE the book!" Yes, you're about to finish the last few pages and physically close the book, but you can (and hopefully will) go through these chapters over and over again to keep learning, refining and living the messages held within.

Every second of the day, I live and breathe the practice of confidence and I am teaching my clients and my children how to do this as well – from leading by example. I am constantly putting myself out there and doing the scary, uncomfortable shit.

I do this knowing I won't always succeed. I won't always get it "right."

I'll piss people off, I'll make mistakes, I'll fail. Remember, it's okay if you don't nail it 24/7. Directly after putting this book down, you'll make a mistake – most likely, you'll go right back to your old subconscious patterns and that's fine in the beginning. Because even though you may go back to doing that, you do it with the awareness that you're doing it, and with *awareness* comes the ability to change.

You'll never unlearn what you've learned in these pages. So your next step is to feel the life you want to create from here on in.

You need to see it, feel it and visualize it, if you're ever going to make what you want a reality.

You need to make a commitment to yourself so that when you finish this book, you have an action plan that you've committed to, not for anyone else, but for yourself – to hold yourself accountable.

If you don't commit to doing the work required, it's your fucking life that you don't get to create. And that should be painful enough.

I mean, imagine you just read this book and then…nothing changes? It just becomes another self-help book you bought in the hope that it would help you become more confident and change your life, but it's sitting there on the shelf, collecting dust. Another book you've "binged." You read it but unfortunately, you didn't action shit.

I'm calling on you to be honest with yourself here! I mean at least keep it real with yourself. Maybe you're not ready to do anything about what you just learned, and if that's the case, then cool.

Maybe you're like I was, and you need some big shit to happen to you to wake you up to the fact that your life is precious and that you're not guaranteed tomorrow? Maybe that's what needs to happen for you.

I get that, because I wasn't ready until I broke my back and lost my husband. I wasn't ready until I spent thousands of dollars on mentors and coaches to start healing all of my shit.

But, if you picked up THIS book, I have a little feeling that you may be ready right now.

That maybe all you need is a little push, a gentle shove, to get you moving in the direction you want to go.

The alternative is this: imagine your life in a year, three years, ten years from now, and NOTHING. CHANGES. The same shit you're currently struggling with now, stays exactly how it is…

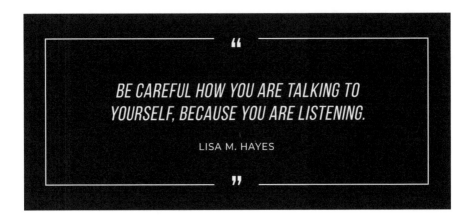

BE CAREFUL HOW YOU ARE TALKING TO YOURSELF, BECAUSE YOU ARE LISTENING.

LISA M. HAYES

Whether you decide to make a change now or not, you are choosing.

So, what's it going to be?

Choose to change your actions with the ideas and tools in this book – or keep telling yourself that confidence isn't available to you? That you're just "not a confident person"?

Do you really want to keep telling yourself that you're never going to be confident or that you don't have what it takes to create confidence?

I mean…WHY?!

Confidence is available to anyone, everyone! So finally commit to stop saying that shit *right now* – like this very moment.

Commit to yourself that you are done calling that bullshit into your future. It stops now.

Call in what you want to have, call in what you *want to experience*.

WHAT I KNOW IS THAT

I DON'T KNOW SHIT.

— ERIKA CRAMER —

I want to end this book by inviting you to create your confidence, because sister, we need you.

The world needs you to remember how incredible you actually are.

Now, more than ever, women need to stand as their fully expressed selves. A lack of confidence may just be the biggest challenge faced by this generation of women and when you play small, you rob others of the gifts you could bring to the world, too.

Are you going to actually DO something with the information in this book?

Approximately 150,000 people die every day.[18] I want you to *really* sit with that – 150,000 people do not wake up and get to have another day, and yet you are here reading these words, alive, breathing. Your heart is beating, what a gift.

If you woke up this morning: **you win**.

Why would you waste another moment of your life not creating your confidence, not doing what lights you up, not being fulfilled, not being happy?

You have the gift of life and yet here you are, wasting your time worrying about how you're not good enough or how people are going to judge you?

Today you're here, tomorrow who knows, and next week? It is definitely not guaranteed – to anyone.

So, what's your story going to be from now on?

There's a story you've been telling yourself about why you haven't achieved the results or outcomes you wanted in your life; this story may even be the reason why you picked up this book.

It's the story of why you *don't* have what you want.

And that's all it is – a story. Not fact. Not truth. Just words floating around in your mind.

Now, you get to rewrite your story.

Now, it's over to you.

How will *your* story end?

What will *you* create?

The pen is in your hand.

The next chapter is on you. 👑

GO FOR
IT NOW.

the future

IS PROMISED
TO NO ONE.

— WAYNE DYER —

ARE YOU READY TO GO DEEPER?

Learn how to create the life you desire.
Be held, seen, guided and supported
as we go deep into the inner work.

Get ready for the ACCOUNTABILITY,
ACTION and A GLOBAL COMMUNITY
of like-minded Queens that have
your back.

Let me coach you for the most
healing year of your life.

The Sistahood is: a year-long coaching
experience designed to help you heal
your past, reclaim your power and
stand as your fully expressed self.

thequeenofconfidence.com

YOU ARE THE
FOUNDATION,

*work
on you*

AND EVERYTHING
YOU CREATE
WILL BENEFIT.

– ERIKA CRAMER –

ACKNOWLEDGMENTS

First and foremost: I acknowledge the Traditional Owners of the land on which I conduct my business, the Wurundjeri People of the Kulin Nation and pay my respects to Elders past and present. I extend respect to the traditional owners of the city of Melbourne, the Boon Wurrung and Woiwurrung (Wurundjeri) people and all the Aboriginal people of this beautiful country I'm now blessed to call my home.

This book was written during the 2020 COVID-19 pandemic while in a stage four lockdown, in Melbourne, Australia.

There are so many people who I need to thank and the most important is my incredible husband, Hamish. Wow, I feel like thanking you could literally be it's very own chapter babe. The countless hours of writing and book brainstorming were possible because of your patience, love and support. It was probably the craziest time to write my first book but as always, you supported me five thousand percent. I know how hectic it was for you to juggle the boys and to not be able to get much work done yourself. I see you and I appreciate you so much honey.

Thank you for listening to me when I sat in self-doubt and worry. Thank you for holding me when I would take a trip down memory lane and end up in tears. You helped me get my stories out, you helped me tap into my heart and soul and I cannot thank you enough. Thank you for seeing me, for loving me as I am and for supporting me to always live in my highest purpose.

Most importantly, thank you for introducing me to this work and helping me heal all the parts of myself I once thought were broken beyond repair. You helped me change my life by being the supportive and caring example of pure love you have always been. How blessed

I am to be doing life with you (again), how blessed our children are to have you as their father and guide. I love you.

To my boys for being so patient with mami as she was glued to the laptop writing this book. Thank you for choosing me to be your mother. Thank you for giving me joy in every single moment of life. Raven, thank you for making me laugh every time you asked me what my book was called and then answered your own question by saying "Confidence is…shit!" Yes, son. Sometimes it is! But no matter how shit it feels, don't ever stop creating it. To Navah, my little man who asked me sixty-seven thousand times to watch Moana while I'd be typing in the corner trying to edit chapters. You are one determined child and I hope you never lose that fire and that persistence. I love you boys so much.

To Jeo, thank you. I know you are always here; I can feel you surrounding our entire family. I know that you have always wanted the best for me. Thank you for teaching me what strength is and that healing is not linear. Thank you for helping me appreciate every second of life my children and my husband have. I celebrate your life and will always carry you into everything I create.

To my mother, wow *mami que te puedo decir mujer! Eres tremenda.* I am so blessed to call you my mother and although we have lived some shit together ma, you have always been my hero. Your resilience, your perseverance and your love never failed. You should be so proud of the women you are. Your heart and your support is always felt. You are my hero mami. I love you so much. *Gracias POR TODO ma.*

To Virma, *ma* what can I say oh my god. You are a literal angel, my guardian all the way through. I can never thank you enough for what you have done for me.

You will always be in my soul and I will forever be grateful that our paths crossed. Thank you for taking me in like a daughter, you are and always will be like a mother to me.

To Michael, *pa*! We love you so much, thank you for supporting us.

To my old social worker Doreen Brooks, my big sister Emily Glick, my case worker Nicole Bouvier, every teacher and foster parent who looked after me, protected me and believed in me. Thank you so much.

To my in-laws, my husbands' parents, Phylis and Ivan, thank you for being angels in this entire process and always looking after us. We are so lucky to have your love and support and even though I was always working, I always felt and continue to feel your encouragement, I love you both. To uncle Matt, our COVID-19 lockdown roomie and my beloved hermano, thank you for looking after the boys so I could write. Thank you for the gin and karaoke nights and most of all for coming home so we could all be together, we love you.

To Tanja, my sista. There are no words, honestly. You saw me, really saw me and for that I am grateful. Thank you for starting me on this journey to healing and responsibility. I lub you prakataaan!

To my darling TQOC team: Niki I adore you and your very existence makes my life a million times better, to Jacqui for your creative brain, to Vass and James for the incredible photography and love you give, to Brianna and Alex – you two legends I am absolutely blessed to call you friends, thank you for everything you have done for our business and our family.

To all of my incredible clients, podcast family, social media followers and Sistahood members especially my OG sistas, this book is for YOU. I wouldn't know what I know if it wasn't for all of you.

Thank you for allowing me to guide, love and support you. To the Sistahood, thank you for trusting me and letting me be a part of your healing journey and life. I love you all so much.

To Sarah Megginson, my rock and creative partner in crime. Holy shit! Sixty thousand words!!! We did it! Sarah, you were like the singer's songwriter and right-hand. We made music together here, sister. We cried. We laughed. We swore and cried some more. It was pure magic. I love that we found each other. To E, thank you so much for your incredible work and support woman, you are amazing!

To the incredible women I was blessed to connect with and feature in this book. To Emma, I love you women and I thank you for always being so real and so uplifting to all women. It's because of watching you birth so powerfully that I too had an incredible home birth. That moment birthed me into the woman I am today. Thanks for being in the book and in my life #BCforlife.

To Lisa, your story and optimism continues to inspire me. You continue to show up and serve no matter what curveball life throws your way. Thank you for your friendship and deep support sista. Thank you for being in the book and for being an incredible example of success. You are such a boss hon.

To Sophie, my love I am so happy that I found you on the 'gram. What a powerful example of confidence, strength and determination you are. Congrats on your legacy and the incredible momentum you have created in the anti-racist movement, you're a thoughtleader and a total inspiration.

To Laticia, *hermana*! Girl what can I say, we got this huh?! Thank you for being a part of my life and this experience. I love you deeply and I am honored to call you a soul sister. Thank you for sharing so openly always and being the example of what sisterhood truly is.

To Samantha, honey you are an absolute legend. How happy I am that we connected and I got to know you. Your son is so lucky to have an incredible mama and woman to look up to. Your work ethic is next level and I am beyond blessed to call you a friend. Thank you all for your contribution to this book.

To five-year-old me, thank you for being such a strong girl. Thank you for teaching me what being strong means. Your resourcefulness and confidence has been the reason I am where I am. I see you Erika. You are great, you are safe and you will change the world.

To Australia, thank you. Being here changed my life. I am grateful for the many opportunities and support this land and it's people have given me.

To Susan Dean and the entire team at Dean Publishing, thank you for all of the amazing work you did to help me birth this book into the world. I am grateful for your countless hours' formatting, editing and working your magic so that this book could be possible.

To Byron Katie and Stephen Mitchell — I am still in awe of your words and deeply powerful contribution to the work that you do on inquiry. Your work has changed my life and given me the gift of loving all that is.

Finally, thank YOU, the reader. Whether you're one of my close friends and sistas (I love you, please know how much you mean to me), my mentors, or a total stranger that somehow attracted this book into your life, I thank you and I honor you for reading this. I hope that you never forget your power.

PODCASTS

ENDNOTES

1 Dyer, Wayne W. Audiobook series from Nightingale-Conant: *How to be a no-limit person; You'll see it when you believe it*. IIIinois, USA.

2 Dispenza, Joe, Dr. Blog: "Change Your Box, Change Your Reality: Part I." Aug 2, 2019. https://blog.drjoedispenza.com/blog/consciousness/change-your-box-change-your-reality-part-i

   Dispenza, Joe, Dr. Blog: "Change Your Box, Change Your Reality: Part II." Aug 16, 2019. https://blog.drjoedispenza.com/blog/consciousness/change-the-box-change-your-reality-part-ii

   Dispenza, Joe, Dr. Blog: "The Habit of Your New Self." Mar 30, 2018. https://blog.drjoedispenza.com/blog/change/the-habit-of-your-new-self

3 Byron, Katie. *The Work of Byron Katie*. https://thework.com

   Katie, Byron. Mitchell, Stephen. *Loving What Is: Four Questions That Can Change Your Life*, Rider, 23rd December 2002. https://thework.com/books

4 *The Dove Global Beauty and Confidence Report*, 2016. Dove Research. https://www.dove.com/au/stories/about-dove/our-research.html

5 Willis, Janine & Todorov, Alexander. (2006). "First Impressions Making Up Your Mind After a 100-Ms Exposure to a Face." *Psychological science*. 17. 592-8. 10.1111/j.1467-9280.2006.01750.x.

6 Seinfeld, Jerry. Stand up recording: "I'm Telling You For the Last Time." YouTube: https://www.youtube.com/watch?v=yQ6giVKp9ec

7 Montonoli, John. National Social Anxiety Center. Blog post "Public Speaking Anxiety and Fear of Brain Freezes." Published

online February 20 2017. Retrieved October 2020. https://nationalsocialanxietycenter.com/2017/02/20/public-speaking-and-fear-of-brain-freezes

8   Angelou, Maya. *O Magazine.* "What I Know For Sure." Oprah. com. Published online: https://www.oprah.com/omagazine/what-i-know-for-sure-gossipMaya Angelou quote

9   Williamson, Marianne. *A Return To Love: Reflections on the Principles of A Course in Miracles.* "Our Deepest Fear." Harper Collins, 13 Oct 2009. For her full poem, go to: https://marianne.com/a-return-to-love

10 Brown, Brené. TEDxHouston. "The power of vulnerability." 2010. https://www.ted.com/talks/brene_brown_the_power_of_vulnerability

11 Vaynerchuk, Gary. *Crushing It! How Great Entrepreneurs Build Their Business and Influence — And How You Can, Too.* Harper Business 2018.

12 Robbins, Tony. "The Power of Tony Robbins Quotes" — Tony Robbins official website: https://www.tonyrobbins.com/tony-robbins-quotes

13 Bilyeu, Tom. Impact Theory Interviews. YouTube interview with Dr Joe Dispenza.
    "How to Unlock the Full Potential of Your Mind | Dr. Joe Dispenza on Impact Theory." July 12, 2018.https://youtu.be/La9oLLoI5Rc

14 Abraham Hicks https://www.abraham-hicks.com

15 Cramer, Erika. The Queen of Confidence. YouTube videos when I first started my business: https://www.youtube.com/channel/UCzgN7oWfbMJVj41xfJLA5Yg

    https://thequeenofconfidence.com

16 Cramer, Erika. "How to Coach Yourself." The 7 steps to coach yourself cheat sheet: https://thequeenofconfidence.com/how-to-coach-yourself

Cramer, Erika. Practice of Confidence cheat sheet: https://thequeenofconfidence.com

17 Robbins, Tony. "The Power of Tony Robbins Quotes" — Tony Robbins official website: https://www.tonyrobbins.com/tony-robbins-quotes

18 Worldometer. https://www.worldometers.info

PERMISSIONS

I'd like to thank Byron Katie and Stephen Mitchell for their kind permission to publish their famous four questions from *The Work*. It means so much to me and your work has changed my life.

ABOUT THE AUTHOR

Known as the Cardi B of the personal development world, Erika Cramer aka The Queen of Confidence is a full-flavored, spicy inspirational speaker and mentor to thousands of women across the globe.

Today, she connects with an engaged global community (The Sistahood) and shares with tens of thousands of women on a daily basis to help empower, encourage and inspire them to step into their confidence.

But it hasn't always been this way. Having survived many traumatic experiences in her youth, Erika spent a number of years searching for love, peace and validation in all the wrong places. She has survived childhood sexual abuse, being brought up in and out of the foster care system, life-altering car accidents and a whole lot of grief and loss.

In the last decade or so, she has been able to turn her life around from one of hopelessness and pain to one of passion, growth and success, after going on her own powerful journey of personal healing.

An international confidence coach, Erika also hosts a five-star rated podcast, *The Confidence Chronicles*, which is in the top 10 of the Australian Apple charts for Mental Health, with 800,000-plus downloads and counting, and listeners in 60-plus countries.

She has created a six-figure global business from absolutely nothing, by mentoring and helping those who have suffered similar life experiences as her own.

Originally from the US, Erika was born in the small town of Framingham, Massachusetts. She has lived all over the US (Orlando, Miami, Boston and LA) due to being in the US Army for a decade, before moving to Sydney, Australia. Since 2011, Erika has called Melbourne, Australia home. She lives near the beach with her husband Hamish and their two sons, Raven and Navah.

Erika's story is one of triumph over adversity and she is full of light, laughter and of course, confidence. Erika is a beaming and beautiful example of how you can heal your personal story to transform trauma into triumph.

Erika is sharing more in her INTERACTIVE book.

See exclusive videos, audios, photos and more...

DOWNLOAD it now at **deanpublishing.com/confidence**